Grace is Not Faceless

Grace is Not Faceless

Reflections on Mary

Ann Loades, CBE

Edited and Introduced by Stephen Burns

DARTON·LONGMAN+TODD

First published in 2021 by
Darton, Longman and Todd Ltd
1 Spencer Court
140–142 Wandsworth High Street
London SW18 4JJ

ISBN: 978-0-232-53420-7

A catalogue record for this book is available from the British Library

Scripture quotations are taken from Revised Standard Version of the Bible, copyright 1952
[2nd edition, 1971] by the Division of Christian Education of the National Council of the
Churches of Christ in the United States of America.

Phototypeset by Kerrypress, St Albans
Printed and bound in Great Britain by Bell & Bain, Glasgow

Contents

Introduction: Graced and Courageous
by Stephen Burns

Grace is Not Faceless is a collection of writings by Ann Loades on Mary. Some readers will wish to launch straight into Ann's own writing, which follows on immediately from this Introduction. Other readers, however, may first choose to begin with the reminders below. The reminders are about Mary in the wider Christian tradition[1] and Anglicanism (Ann's tradition) in particular. Some notes then set Ann's writing on Mary in relation to her wider work, as well as among Anglicans like and unlike herself, so providing different pathways to Ann's writing itself.

1. Mary

Gospels

As Beverley Roberts Gaventa—who has produced the main work on Mary in scripture[2]—notes, 'The New Testament offers only fleeting glimpses of Mary'.[3] She is not a major figure in the canonical gospels. In fact, bar Mark 6:3, the first gospel is silent about her. In Matthew, though, she gains a few entries: 1:16 includes her name in Jesus' genealogy; 1:18-25 presents her being spoken of in Joseph's dream, and 1:27 calls her 'virgin'/'young woman'. In Matthew 12:46-50 she tries to speak to Jesus; and she is mentioned again in 13:58. Beverly Roberts Gaventa suggests that in Matthew's gospel Mary is 'threatened and threatening'. She is threatened in that she is vulnerable to both Herod and Joseph (who may reject her), and she is threatening in so far as she is embroiled in secrets, and, potentially, a threat (if she says 'no') to God's plan.

In Luke's gospel, Mary is a major figure in the birth narrative of 1:5-2:52. Indeed, she might even be imagined as a source of the narrative, given its apparent insights into her thoughts. She wants—but seems to fail—to speak to Jesus in 8:19-21 (cf. Matt. 12:46-50), she is mentioned indirectly in 11:27-28, and in Luke's second volume, Acts of the Apostles, she is depicted as being present at Pentecost (Acts 1:4). Beverly Roberts Gaventa suggests that the Lucan portrayal of Mary has a three-fold focus: disciple, prophet, and mother. She is disciple (even 'slave' [Luke 1:38]—with the New Testament Greek also meaning 'child', of God), saying 'let it be to me according to your word' in response to the divine messenger who visits her. She is prophet, singing the *Magnificat* (Luke 1:46-55)—also known as the 'Canticle of Mary' or, in the Orthodox tradition, 'Ode of the *Theotokos*'— her song of praise to God who looks upon and lifts up the lowly, evoked in response to her relative Elizabeth's acclamation, 'Blessed are you among women, and blessed is the fruit of your womb' (Luke 1:42). And she is of course mother, with Luke 1:43 the origin of the later widespread affirmation of her as *Theotokos*, that is 'God-bearer', or 'Mother of God'.

John's gospel then has two foci on Mary, in John 2:1-11 and 19:25-27. Curiously John never mentions her by name, but refers to her as either 'woman' or 'mother'—perhaps as part of an anti-Docetic agenda, Docetism being a heresy that Christ's body was only seemingly and not really fully human. Stories about the woman who was his mother might have been meant to contest this idea. In any case, Gaventa's moniker for Mary in the Fourth Gospel is: 'Cana and the Cross'.

As significant for doctrine about Mary as any canonical gospel is a particular *non*-canonical text: *The Protoevangelium of James*, a text with second-century origins, is unlike its non-canonical contemporaries as well as canonical counterparts in being unusually focused on the figure of Mary. It is *The Protoevangelium of James* that yields to the Christian tradition the names of Mary's parents (Anna and Joachim). It gives an account of her privileged family (contra the canon). It tells the story of Mary's cloistering by Anna and Mary's childhood in the temple, weaving scarlet and purple. It suggests Mary's marriage to Joseph four years before the birth of Jesus (contra the canon again); and it identifies the place of her giving birth to Jesus as a cave (once more, contra the canon). *The Protoevangelium of James* also portrays Jesus' first miracle not as making wine at the wedding of Cana (as John 2), but the healing of Salome's hand. Perhaps most importantly for later doctrine, it claims Mary's virgin state as she gave birth to Jesus.[4]

Feasts

Anna and Joachim are just two of the saints amongst whom, in Catholic tradition at least, Jesus is imagined as being 'always in company', 'never see[n] alone'.[5] Mary is singled out amongst the saints in every single Roman

Catholic eucharistic prayer, and she is the central focus of twelve days in the *sanctorale*, or calendar of the saints, of the Roman Church.[6] Christmastide entries into the calendar were first to emerge (in the fifth century, and it seems at first on December 26);[7] in the Roman Catholic tradition, January 1 remains, as it has long been, a 'Solemnity of Mary'—whereas by contrast, in Protestant traditions, it is more typically given to 'The Naming and Circumcision of Jesus', as in the Church of England's *Common Worship*. (A wider range of tradition at large, though, may allow for some sort of Marian focus in the season of Advent, with its emphasis on preparing for Christ's arrival.) In some contexts—and notably narratives of the fifth-century empress Pulcheria—devotions to do with nativity explicitly involved the idea that others might 'give birth to God mystically', 'in the soul',[8] as Mary had done in her body.

Inclusion of days dedicated to Mary in the Christmas calendar was closely followed by a day given to the Feast of the Assumption (August 15), which was widespread by the sixth century. As Johannine language may have had anti-Docetic targets, fifth-century Marian mysticism had in its sights Nestorianism. Nestorius had famously declared that 'God is not a baby two or three months old', with his views of Christ's less-than-full humanity a provocation for the Council of Ephesus in 431. In Constantinople, Pulcheria had named new church buildings after Mary as another part of her commendation of Marian devotion, and the ways in which Nestorius' ideas upset devotees of Mary seems to have been key to his downfall. While contemporaneous 'orthodox' preachers in Pulcheria's circle proclaimed 'let nature leap for joy', 'all humanity dance'—and not least 'women be honoured'[9]— on account of Mary, creedal statements emerging from the Councils of Ephesus and Chalcedon (451) brought forward what may be the more restrained but nonetheless determined ascription: *Theotokos*, 'Mother of God'—that is, more than merely 'mother of the man'. Lavish sermonising continued to flourish, with Mary declared, on defeat of Nestorius' views, as 'venerable treasure of all the world, the inextinguishable lamp, the crown of virginity, the sceptre of orthodoxy, the indestructible temple, the container of the Uncontainable, the Mother and Virgin, the source of the one of whom it is said in the holy Gospels, "Blessed is he who comes in the name of the Lord"'.[10] Note, not least, the ascription, 'sceptre of orthodoxy'. Doctrinal definition and overflowing honour most likely both reflect longstanding devotion to Mary, with the first extant prayer addressed to Mary, the *sub tuum*, addressing her as 'Mother of God', being third century.

Prayer

Whatever Marian devotions are this old, others took strong hold later: notably the rosary, a version of which has some roots in the twelfth-century, when it was popularised in association with St Dominic (1170-1221), whose legend has him receiving a vision of Mary in which, along with her pressed milk, he is given instructions for the rosary's use.[11] Over time, use of the rosary has evolved, to focus on a skein of mysteries in the life of Jesus, and in recent times it has been especially commended by Pope John Paul II, who spoke of it as a means by which a believer can 'sit at the school of Mary and [be] led to contemplate the beauty on the face of Christ and to experience the depth of his love'.[12] John Paul II also introduced a new focus to meditation on the life of Christ using the rosary, setting alongside 'joyful mysteries' of Christ's birth (annunciation, visitation, nativity, presentation, and being found in the temple aged 12), 'sorrowful mysteries' of his passion (agony, scourging, crowning with thorns, cross-carrying, and crucifixion) and 'glorious mysteries' of his (and Mary's) risen life (his resurrection and ascension, Pentecost, her assumption and her crowning as queen of heaven), an additional new emphasis on 'luminous mysteries' (baptism, Cana, proclamation of the divine reign, transfiguration, and eucharist). Notably, perhaps because of its invitation to scriptural imagination, the rosary has been amenable to at least some Protestants.[13]

Other devotions to Mary meld other scriptural allusions in creative ways—a prime example being the mid-sixteenth century Litany of Loreto with its cascade of images: 'Mirror of justice, Seat of wisdom, Cause of our joy', ' 'Mystical rose … House of gold, Ark of the covenant', 'Refuge' and 'help'—as she had already long been named by the *sub tuum*, and 'Queen': of angels, prophets, apostles, all saints, and families. If this litany has Italian origins, the *sanctorale* associates Mary with various places (for example, Lourdes, France), and so do a skein of apparitions in other places: Guadalupe, Mexico (1531), Fatima, Portugal (1917), Kibeho, Rwanda (1981) and Medjugorje, Yugoslavia (now Croatia) (1981), amongst them.

Anglicanism

The Anglican tradition has entered into some of this heritage and trajectory, but has not done so uniformly. In the Reformation-era, Marian shrines were destroyed, pilgrimages suppressed, rosaries banned, the Hail Mary removed from common prayer, with, therein, an oscillating range of reference to Mary in authorised prayer. The first vernacular service to be published was the Litany, in 1544, and that included an invocation, 'Holy

Virgin Mary, Mother of God our Saviour Jesus Christ, pray for us', though this was removed from the first full prayer book, of 1549. The 1549 Book of Common Prayer (BCP) did name Mary in the prayers of the people, but had its strongest Marian focus in a commemoration in communion giving 'high praise and hearty thanks, for the wonderful grace and virtue declared in all thy Saints from the beginning of the world: And chiefly for the glorious and most Blessed Virgin Mary, Mother of thy Son ...'. That 1549 book also referred to—but did not address—Mary as 'our Lady'. And notably, it did not include a calendar day for the Assumption.[14] The next prayer book, of 1552, went much further in a reforming direction, removing the 1549 eucharistic reference to Mary, and indeed excluding her name and reference to the saints.

However, whatever prayer books have or have not allowed, Marian devotion has oftentimes been present among Anglicans: at the very least, Mary continued to be present in the environment of Anglican worship in churches named after her, (a few surviving) statues and (much more) stained glass, in major festivals (two were deemed 'biblical': Annunciation and Purification) as well as three lesser festivals (visitation, nativity and *her* conception, which is marked in the calendar of the BCP of 1662, on 8 December). Mary has perhaps remained most present to Anglicans, however, via the *Magnificat*—which is a default text in the 1662 BCP evening service, and remains a key part of Evensong in some Anglican contexts—that is, at least where Evensong prevails these days.[15] As Paul Williams asserts, 'The place of the Virgin Mary in Anglican tradition is assured because of Mary's place in the Gospel tradition',[16] notwithstanding the 'scant' character of the gospels' witness with regard to her.

Mary became altogether more significant in Anglicanism through the Oxford Movement, which incrementally drew in aspects of Roman devotion: for example, use of litanies of invocation, with the subtle addition of the word 'may' (so, 'N., pray for us' becomes 'May N. pray for us'). Notably, Oxford Movement personality John Keble (1792-1866) published a poem posthumously, 'Mother Out of Sight', which speaks of saying 'Ave' to Mary as 'children come ... to elders in some happy home'.[17]

Immaculate Conception, Glorious Assumption
The date of Keble's poem (it was written in 1846) is close to Pope Pius IX's promulgation of the dogma of the Immaculate Conception on 8 December 1854, and the first of two Roman dogmas that form what have sometimes been identified as the 'most awkward' differences between Anglican and

Roman Catholic perspectives.[18] Indeed, of the two dogmas, the Immaculate Conception has been said to be 'the most problematic' of all.[19] This dogma asserts that Mary was, 'from the first moment of her conception, by the singular grace and privilege of almighty God and in view of the merits of Jesus Christ the Saviour of the human race, preserved immune from all stain of original sin'. This dogma protects Mary from sin altogether, from the first, as well as after her consent to, and giving birth to Jesus, hence 'perpetually' virgin. Most Protestants might now perhaps regard the dogma as unconfirmed by scripture, though many figures in Protestant thought (Martin Luther, John Calvin, the Wesley brothers, and various Anglican divines) apparently all assented to the content of the doctrine, albeit evidently often resistant to what they saw as 'misdirected' devotional practices associated with it.

The Assumption of Mary into heaven is the second of the two dogmas. It was promulgated by Pope Pius XII in 1950—as sociologist Peter Berger has noted, 'on the very eve of Sputnik as it were'.[20] This dogma asserts that 'the Immaculate Mother of God, the ever Virgin Mary, having completed the course of her earthly life, was assumed body and soul into heavenly glory'. If the Immaculate Conception was sometimes tracked back to *The Protoevangelium of James*, the Assumption was related to a fourth-century document, *De Obitu S. Dominae*. Yet more influential on the development and reception of the idea of Mary's assumption was St John of Damascus who wrote that 'Mary died in the presence of all the apostles, but [ ] her tomb, when upon the request of St Thomas, was found empty', leading the apostles to conclude that her body was taken to heaven. Though this story is not scriptural, it places Mary alongside scriptural figures like Enoch (Genesis 5:24) and Elijah (2 Kings 2:11). Revelation 12's imagery of a woman clothed with the sun gave the doctrine some pictorial collateral, funding the notion of Mary as Queen of Heaven, as found in the Litany of Loreto and many other sources of Catholic devotion.

Bi-lateral ecumenical dialogue between Anglicans and Roman Catholics, through the Anglican-Roman Catholic International Commission (ARCIC), produced a document in 2005, *Mary: Grace and Hope in Christ*. The document suggests that Anglicans might both recognise the Immaculate Conception and the Assumption as consonant with scripture and acknowledge a common faith with Roman Catholics concerning Mary. This may be so, the document posits, at least if they start with scriptural affirmation of fullness of grace (Luke 1:28) in Mary, and then insert this affirmation into a wider doctrine of predestination (drawn from Romans

8:30) turned to speak of Mary's foreknown role to be the Mother of God. Key for the ARCIC statement, the Assumption celebrates God's action in Mary, taking her into divine glory, whilst the Immaculate Conception means that Mary has need of Christ as saviour, but that Christ's salvation is, as it were, 'reached "back"'[21] to her, so that the redemption of the cross is in her 'out of sequence', with God's glory filling her from the beginning.

Whatever the historicity of the dogmas, or indeed the cogency of their various expressions, their pastoral import, and reasons for their reception, might, perhaps, be discerned via note of the day in 1954 on which the Assumption was promulgated: 1 November, that is, in the liturgical calendar, All Saints' Day. The dogmas may, in a generous reading, be understood as being, in some sense, about all people: for although they give special honour to Mary, they witness to a grace that the Christian tradition alleges is for all. Interestingly, feminist theologians are among those who hold this conviction most strongly, a vivid example being Ivone Gebara and Clara Bingemer in their 'dogmatics of the poor', Mary: *Mother of God, Mother of Poor*, a book that relentlessly seeks and sees Mary as the clue that 'God's glory shine[s] on what is regarded as insignificant, degrading, or marginal'.[22] So the Immaculate Conception reveals the 'yearnings and longings, the divine proposal for humankind, already achieved',[23] 'God's preference for the humblest, the littlest, and the most oppressed',[24] and so foreshadows what is true of all the needy. And Mary's Assumption is the 'complete fulfilment of the whole woman, Mary', an image of the final destiny to which all are called, and so a 'hope-inspiring horizon'.[25] To affirm and 'exalt Mary, immaculately conceived, assumed into heaven' as these doctrines do is, for Gebara and Bingemer, to insist that 'in exalting her, they exalt precisely her poverty, her dispossession ...',[26] and so they stir hope that God's reign can indeed be achieved 'on this poor earth'.

2. Ann

Searching for lost coins, etc.
Ann Loades is perhaps best-known for her work in feminist theology:[27] *Searching for Lost Coins* (1987)[28] was the first monograph on feminist theology to emerge from a British university-based academic. It was in *Searching for Lost Coins* that Ann Loades first wrote about Mary, uncluttering traditions about the mother of Jesus from those about Mary of Magdala. This was in a chapter called 'god/goddess' that also discussed 'feminine' images of the divine, in which Ann asserted a view she has

continued to hold, that naming towards God as 'mother' is not in and of itself transformative, unless allied to real efforts to change things for the better for women. Some 'traditional' language — for example, 'Lord' — may in fact remain valuable for 'put[ting] even the best "lords" of this world in their places'.[29] Hence, it is political. Ann later published *Feminist Theology: A Reader* (1990),[30] a collection that was instrumental in introducing many readers to feminist theology, lifting up voices from the movement then gathering force from around the North Atlantic.[31] One extract included in the reader, by Merry Weisner, focused on Mary: 'Luther and Women: The Death of Two Marys'. A decade later came *Feminist Theology: Voices from the Past* (2000).[32] Whereas *Searching for Lost Coins* had ranged across the work of many authors (Elizabeth Cady Stanton, Mary Daly, Emily Dickinson, Helen Waddell, Simone Weil, among various others), *Voices from the Past* explored in detail the thought of just three women: Mary Wollstonecraft, Josephine Butler and Dorothy L. Sayers. None of these three forebears in Ann Loades' own Anglican tradition made Mary a particular focus in their work, and so Mary does not appear in that book.[33]

Between 1990 and 2000, though, Ann Loades herself made Mary central in some of her own other writing. So in 1990 she contributed an essay 'The Virgin Mary in the Feminist Quest' to a collection, *After Eve*.[34] In this, Ann engaged with the teaching on Mary in the Roman Catholic Church's Second Vatican Council and some subsequent papal statements, noting some problems from her feminist perspective. Ann also took up invitations to speak to the Ecumenical Society of the Blessed Virgin Mary (ESBVM), resulting in further publications pushing forward exploration of—sometimes pushing back on—the Roman Church's teaching.[35] Then in 2000, Ann addressed the International Mariological-Marian Congress in Rome, on the position of Mary in Anglicanism, and in which she amongst other things considered creedal formulations on Christ's conception by Mary and the Holy Spirit.[36] This address represented a turn in Ann's work to Marian thought in the Anglican tradition and served as a precursor to later assessment of the official ARCIC dialogue on Mary.

In several pieces of Ann's work on Mary, then, one can see main lines and key aspects of recent Roman Catholic and Anglican thinking on Mary. But the vista is bigger than that given by official representatives of those churches' Marian doctrine, because Ann also explores critique of that by feminists in those churches. For example, the views of Elizabeth Johnson and Tina Beattie—two Roman Catholic theologians whose main Marian work was published in the early years of the new millennium—are crucial in influencing Ann's own views as they emerge over time, as can be seen especially in another essay of Ann's, 'Mary: Bone of Contention' (2009),[37] from a book on 'women in the New Testament and their afterlives'. In gathering these essays, *Grace is Not Faceless* therefore provides a wider and critical view of official teaching on Mary by the churches in the last half-century, pointing up clear gaps where official teaching has not absorbed what it, in Ann's view, might and should have learned from Christian feminists. As Ann puts things rather forcefully in 'Bone of Contention', their feminist perspectives are 'completely ignored by the [ARCIC's *Mary: Grace and Hope in Christ*], presumably because [feminist perspectives] are not yet deemed to be part of the "tradition". The first essays in this book, then, explore ecclesial teaching, and feminist Marian thinkers' ideas, and work into the space between them.

Alongside these essays, *Grace is Not Faceless* adds some others. 'The Nativity in Recent Poetry' (2009), written for a collection on 'new perspectives on the nativity',[38] attends to the art-form referenced in its title, whereas 'Mary: For Now' (2019), previously unpublished, provides much wider angles on the contemporary arts that might inform Marian doctrine and devotion at the present time. Poetry has been present in Ann's work at least since *Searching for Lost Coins*, with the rationale for its presence articulated succinctly in that book: 'I do not conceive resources for theological reflection in too narrow terms'.[39] In its use of poetry, this essay is characteristic of a number of other pieces of her writing.[40] The new essay on wider art forms reflects her more recent work on a whole variety of media,[41] especially the novel form, focusing on the work of Evelyn Underhill and Dorothy L. Sayers, before exploring the biblical studies by Margaret Barker on the way to an ending that engages with contemporary trauma theory.

All of these essays are followed by a couple of Ann's sermons on Mary, one which was preached at St Paul's Cathedral, London, and another given at the All Saints Scottish Episcopal Church, St Andrews. These enrich the genres in which Ann Loades has thought and spoken about Mary, rounding out the picture of Ann's own Marian convictions, and they are complemented in turn by a commentary commissioned from her to accompany the British Royal Mail's stamps for Christmas 2019. These stamps placed Ann's texts in a presentation pack[42] alongside images where they would inevitably reach far wider than to audiences of professional theologians, ecumenical gatherings, feminist circles, or particular assemblies of worship. Included here is the full text Ann contributed to the presentation pack, from which fragments appeared on the stamps themselves.

More voices

Ann is among a small number of Anglicans who have made Mary a focus of their work in recent years, A. M. (Donald) Allchin, Roger Greenacre, John Macquarrie and Nicola Slee being notable among those who have shared a keen interest in her. The distinctiveness of Ann's voice becomes clear by some comparison of their contributions.

John Macquarrie (1919-2007), a professional theologian like Ann, tackles amongst other things the Roman dogmas head on in order to make something of them, and he does so with an ecumenical concern which his title reflects: *Mary for All Christians*.[43] His book, like this one, also collects papers presented over a period of time, some of which also began life as talks to the ESBVM. The first chapter of Macquarrie's book is on 'God and the feminine', from 1975, and while affirming that 'the movement toward greater equality' is an 'aspect' of 'the sexual revolution' that 'must commend itself to Christians', it makes no engagement with the then nascent movement of feminist theology. Nor do figures associated with that movement appear in chapters of the book that have later origins, when the movement had grown in strength.

Roger Greenacre (1931-2011), like Macquarrie, was an ordained priest, though working from posts in parishes and cathedrals and not universities. Like Macquarrie's book *Mary for All Christians*, Greenacre's *Maiden, Mother and Queen* (published posthumously in 2013) also incorporates addresses to the ESBVM, and its focus is suggested by the book's subtitle: 'Mary in the Anglican tradition', albeit also—like Macquarrie—with ecumenical dialogue in view. Just as Macquarrie sees 'the sexual revolution as an ambiguous development', Greenacre names 'the feminist movement' as 'ambiguous', indeed sometimes 'radically hostile', not just to 'traditional Mariology' but to 'Christian orthodoxy'. However, Greenacre states a view that 'a lot of [the feminist movement] has been positive' as a stimulus to some to explore the place of Mary in Christian theology and spirituality. It is notable, then, that of the more-than-ten-page index, Mary is one of very few women mentioned—others being the biblical Elizabeth (numerous references), Queen Elizabeth I (one reference), and Cinderella (two references). So the feminist movement does not really show up. There are, however, multiple references to 'women, ordination of', about which Greenacre remained 'agnostic' and 'sad'. He would certainly not have agreed with Ann Loades' position on the ordination of women to the episcopate, the Church of England working group on which she joined only on the clear proviso that her view of women's aptness to be in the order was made known from the start.[44]

Donald Allchin (1930-2010), like Greenacre, was a priest who did theological work from parishes and cathedrals. Allchin's learned *The Joy of All Creation* [45] explores Mary in Anglican tradition, providing highly insightful views of a range of Anglican forebears. Yet it too elides feminist theologians. In fact, with respect to the twentieth-century, Allchin discusses no theologians at all, at least not professional ones, but focuses exclusively on the work of poets: so the Welsh wordsmith Euros Bowen as well as perhaps more widely-known Scot Edwin Muir and American T. S. Eliot are his foci.[46]

Though Nicola Slee is also prolific in prose, her work *The Book of Mary*[47] is largely a book of poems, albeit with extensive introduction and notes that locate the theological issues at play in her verses. Nicola Slee, like Ann Loades, is an Anglican laywoman. And whereas Allchin, Greenacre and Macquarrie are disengaged from feminist perspectives, like Ann's work, Nicola Slee's absorbs, employs and advances them.[48] In Slee's case, she sometimes makes direct reference to the writings of feminist theologians in her poetry: so, for example, one chapter of Slee's *Book of Mary* is called 'Truly Our Sister', after Elizabeth Johnson's major volume on Mary, and the poem 'Searching the Faces of Maria' expands an epitaph of Marcella Althaus-Reid.[49]

In this company, Ann's work yields a particular sense of the richness of the tradition, in which, whatsoever some contemporary officials say, includes feminist perspectives, and ideas about what might be done to contest and address the persistent imperviousness to feminist insights of church teaching on Mary. At the same time, we see the appeal of Mary via Ann's capacity to find resources in the tradition that have not been valued as they ought to be. That is, she manifests the practice of 'searching for lost coins', finding treasures waiting to be claimed. Just one example, as readers will see in the following pages, is in relation to depictions of Mary in art of the Rabula Gospels. So Ann shows in her own way something of how in Nicola Slee's terms Mary might be a 'mansion', inviting endless exploration, and still with ability to surprise. As Slee puts things: 'the whole vast mansion' of Mary 'is humming, / a huge belly gestating numerous births'[50]—words from her poem 'The Mansion of Mary', itself a mediation on Kathleen Norris' conviction that 'there is a lot of room in Mary'. This is elaborated by Slee in her sense that 'Mary herself, in all her forms and guises, is a fecund source of life. Whatever difficulties there may be in reclaiming Mary as a woman who can inspire contemporary women and men, I believe there is so much that is life-giving and creative … While there is a need to repudiate, for Mary and for us to say "no" to much of what we have inherited, there is also much to affirm, in the spirit of Mary's radical and faithful "yes" to God'.[51]

Across Ann Loades' essays, another distinctive and recurring emphasis is the sheer courage of Mary's assent to the incarnation, indeed, to quote as Ann does at one point from Denise Levertov's poetry, 'courage unparalleled'. And as, over the course of *Grace is Not Faceless*, Ann draws several times on the phrase which gives this book its title—a pithy idiom of Dominican, Cornelius Ernst — it can reasonably be concluded that this too distils more of Ann's own central convictions about Mary. Seemingly affecting for her, this image also extends an invitation to readers to consider how Mary in the first instance, but others in their turn, might manifest the mystery to which Mary gives her courageous assent.

NOTES TO INTRODUCTION

[1] I teach on Mary to a mixed cohort in an ecumenical university. So my class gathers longstanding devotees to Mary from Roman Catholic formation around the world alongside those from a variety of Protestant traditions. The biblical material on Mary, such as it is, is typically unknown or little-known to some, while extra-canonical traditions and devotions may be completely new to the same or other students. My notes may help to orient such readers to Ann Loades' explorations which follow.

[2] Beverly Gaventa, *Mary: Glimpses of the Mother of Jesus* (Columbia, S.C.: University of South Carolina Press, 1995).

[3] Gaventa, *Mary: Glimpses,* p. 100. Also, 'slender' (pp. 4, 9), 'scant' (pp. 29, 60, 73), 'glimpses' (title, p. 2).

[4] See Gaventa, *Mary: Glimpses,* for full text and commentary. See also, for background, Fred Lapham, *An Introduction to the New Testament Apocrypha* (London: Continuum, 2003), and for wider views of *The Protoevangelium of James* alongside like-kind texts, J. K. Elliot, *The Apocryphal Jesus: Legends of the Early Church* (Oxford: Oxford University Press, 1996) and in particular Chris Maunder, 'Mary in the New Testament and Apocrypha', in Sarah Jane Boss, ed., *Mary: The Complete Resource* (Oxford: Oxford University Press, 2007), pp. 11-46.

[5] Charles Sherlock and Peter Cross, 'The Liturgical Commemoration of the Blessed Virgin Mary in the Roman Catholic Church and the Anglican Communion', in Adelbert Denaux and Nicholas Sagovsky, eds, *Studying Mary: The Virgin Mary in Anglican and Catholic Theology and Devotion* (London: T & T Clark, 2008), pp. 222-243, at p. 222.

[6] December 8: Immaculate Conception, January 1: Solemnity of Mary, March 25: Annunciation, and August 15: Assumption of Our Lady are major feast days. February 2: Presentation, May 31: Visitation, September 8: Nativity of Our Lady, and September 15: Our Lady of Sorrows are lesser feasts. February 11: Our Lady of Lourdes, July 16: Our Lady of Carmel, August 5: Dedication of Santa Maria Maggiore, and October 7: Our Lady of the Rosary are commemorations. For those unfamiliar with the schema, the first cluster are considered of most importance, the latter cluster relatively less so.

[7] Richard Price, 'Theotokos: The Title and its Significance in Doctrine and Devotion', in Sarah Jane Boss, ed., *Mary: The Complete Resource* (London: Continuum, 2007), 56-73, at p. 59.

[8] See discussion in Paul Bradshaw and Maxwell Johnson, *The Origins of Feasts, Fasts and Seasons in Early Christianity* (London: SPCK, 2011), pp. 196-214, elaborated in Maxwell Johnson, *Praying and Believing in Early Christianity: The Interplay Between Christian Worship and Doctrine* (Collegeville, Minn.: Liturgical Press, 2013).

[9] Price, 'Theotokos', p. 59.

[10] Price, 'Theotokos', p. 62.

[11] See Sarah Jane Boss, 'Telling the Beads', in Sarah Jane Boss, ed., *Mary: The Complete Resource* (London: Continuum, 2007), pp. 385-394.

[12] See Francesca Murphy, 'Immaculate Mary: The Ecclesial Mariology of Hans Urs von Balthasar', in Sarah Jane Boss, ed., *Mary: The Complete Resource* (London: Continuum, 2007), pp. 300-313, at p. 312.

[13] Note, for example, (Methodist) Neville Ward's *Five for Sorrow, Ten for Joy* (London: Epworth Press, 1971; reprinted by the Episcopal Church press Cowley in 2005). Until the fourteenth century, only the scriptural sentence was used; see Boss, 'Telling the Beads', p. 390.

[14] In the Church of England's *Common Worship* of 2000, August 15 was restored as the principal Marian feast, though *Common Worship* does not mention the Assumption, whilst hinting at it, perhaps, in asking God that 'we who are redeemed by [Christ's] blood / may share with [Mary] in the glory of your eternal kingdom'. Through the latter part of the twentieth century, following South African revision in 1954 which had August 15 as 'The Falling Asleep of the Blessed Virgin Mary', other churches of the Anglican Communion have again marked this day.

[15] In some Anglican traditions around the world, the *Magnificat* remains a default text in Evening Prayer; in others, it is one among a range of options. In the new plethora of forms for everyday prayer in the Anglican tradition emerging at the present time, it may not be present regularly, if at all. See Stephen Burns, "'Learning Again and Again to Pray": Anglican Forms of Daily Prayer, 1979-2014,' *Journal of Anglican Studies* 15 (2017): 9-36.

[16] Paul Williams, 'The Virgin Mary in Anglican Tradition', in Sarah Jane Boss, ed., *Mary: The Complete Resource* (London: Continuum, 2007), pp. 314-339, at p. 315.

[17] See discussion in Williams, 'Anglican Tradition', and Roger Greenacre, *Maiden, Mother, Queen: Mary in the Anglican Tradition* (Norwich: Canterbury Press, 2013), pp. 115-130.

[18] Harriet Harris, 'A Feminist Response to ARCIC's Mary: Grace and Hope in Christ', in *GS Misc 872—Mary: Grace and Hope in Christ (ARCIC II): Essays by the Faith and Order Advisory Group of the Church of England* (London: 2008), pp. 38-47, at p.42.

[19] Harris, 'Feminist Response', p. 43.

[20] Peter Berger, *A Rumour of Angels: Modern Society and the Rediscovery of the Supernatural* (New York, N.Y.: Anchor, 1970), p. 49.

[21] ARCIC, *Mary: Grace and Hope in Christ*, para. 59 (cf. para. 52). See Adelbert Denaux, Nicholas Sagovsky and Charles Sherlock, eds, *Looking Towards a Church Fully Reconciled: The Final Report of the Anglican-Roman Catholic International Commission 1983-2005 (ARCIC II)* (London: SPCK, 2016), p. 210; cf. p. 206.

[22] Ivone Gebara and Maria Clara Bingemer, *Mary: Mother of God, Mother of the Poor* (Maryknoll, N.Y.: Orbis, 1989), p. 92. Note that Gebara and Bingemer's book is subject to critique by a later Latin American feminist theologian, Marcella Althaus-Reid, in her *Indecent Theology* (London: Routledge, 2000), with its contention that Latin American women do not necessarily identify with Mary because Mary represents a 'sexual decency' that many woman cannot attain.

[23] Gebara and Bingemer, *Mary*, p. 112.

[24] Gebara and Bingemer, *Mary*, p. 113.

[25] Gebara and Bingemer, *Mary*, p. 118.

[26] Gebara and Bingemer, *Mary*, p. 93.

[27] See Stephen Burns, 'Ann Loades (1938 -)', in Stephen Burns, Bryan Cones and James Tengatenga, eds, *Twentieth-century Anglican Theologians* (Chicester: Wiley-Blackwell, 2020), 157-166.

[28] Ann Loades, *Searching for Lost Coins: Explorations in Christianity and Feminism* (London: SPCK, 1987).

[29] Ann Loades, 'Finding New Sense in the Sacramental', in Geoffrey Rowell and Christine Hall, eds, *The Gestures of God: Explorations in Sacramentality* (London: Continuum, 2004), 161-172, p. 171.

[30] Ann Loades, *Feminist Theology: A Reader* (London: SPCK, 1990).

[31] It was complemented by a volume edited by Ursula King, *Feminist Theology from The Third World* (London: SPCK, 1994).

[32] Ann Loades, *Feminist Theology: Voices from the Past* (Oxford: Polity/Routledge, 2000).

[33] Alongside these three, Evelyn Underhill stands as a major figure for Ann's attention; see Ann Loades, *Evelyn Underhill* (London: Fount, 1997). A recent essay on Underhill's novels, which are much less well-known than Underhill's writing on, say, *Mysticism* or *Worship*, reveals the persistent presence of Marian imagery in Underhill's scenes. See Ann Loades, 'Evelyn Underhill (1875-1941): Mysticism in Fiction', in Judith Maltby and Alison Shell, eds, *Anglican Women Novelists* (London: Continuum, 2019), pp. 73-86.

[34] Ann Loades, 'The Virgin Mary and the Feminist Quest', in Janet Martin Soskice, ed., *After Eve: Women, Theology and the Christian Tradition* (London: Collins, 1990), pp. 156-178.

[35] Ann Loades, 'Feminist Theology: A View of Mary', in William McLoughlin and Jill Pinnock, eds, *Mary is for Everyone: Essays on Mary and Ecumenism* (Leominster: Gracewing, 1997), pp. 32-40.

[36] Ann Loades, 'The Position of the Anglican Communion Regarding the Trinity and Mary', *New Blackfriars* 82 (2001): 364-374.

[37] Ann Loades, 'Mary: Bone of Contention', Christine E. Joynes and Christopher C. Rowland, eds, *From the Margins 2: Women of the New Testament and their Afterlives* (Sheffield: Pheonix, 2009), pp. 53-66.

[38] Ann Loades, 'The Nativity in Recent British Poetry', in Jeremy Corley, ed., *New Perspectives on the Nativity* (London: Continuum, 2009), pp. 148-163.

[39] Loades, *Searching*, p. 15.

[40] Notably, Ann Loades, 'Word and Sacrament: Recovering Integrity', in Neil Brown and Robert Gasgone, eds, *Faith in the Public Forum* (Adelaide: Openbook, 2000), pp. 28-46.

[41] Ann Loades, 'Lazarus Without Limits: Scripture, Tradition, and the Cultural Life of a Text', *International Journal for the Study of the Christian Church* 18 (2018): 252-264; Ann Loades, 'Some Straws in the Wind: Reflections Towards Theological Engagement with Theatre Dance', Christopher R. Brewer, ed., *Christian Theology and the Transformation of Natural Religion: From Incarnation to Sacramentality—Essays in Honour of David Brown* (Leuven: Brill, 2018), pp. 193-205.

[42] *www.royalmail.com/stamps*

[43] John Macquarrie, *Mary for All Christians* (London: Collins, 1991).

[44] Ann Loades, 'Women in the Episcopate?' *Anvil* 21 (2004): 113-119.

[45] A. M. Allchin, *The Joy of All Creation: An Anglican Meditation on the Place of Mary* (London: New City Press, [2] 1993).

[46] Note also Gordon Wakefield, 'The Blessed Virgin Mary in Some Modern Poets', in William McLoughlin and Jill Pinnock, eds, *Mary is for Everyone: Essays on Mary and Ecumenism* (Leominster: Gracewing, 1997), pp. 294-303.

[47] Nicola Slee, *The Book of Mary* (London: SPCK, 2007), the middle of a series of books of poems: *Praying Like a Woman* (London: SPCK, 2004) and *Seeking the Risen Christa* (London: SPCK, 2011).

[48] An essay of Nicola Slee's also features in *Feminist Theology: A Reader.*

[49] Ch. 4 in 'Truly Our Sister', Ch. 10, 'Searching for the Faces of Maria'—a line from Marcella Althaus-Reid, *From Feminist Theology to Indecent Theology* (London: SCM Press, 2004), p. 43.

[50] Slee, *Book of Mary*, p. 3.

[51] Slee, *Book of Mary*, p. 12.

1

The Virgin Mary and the Feminist Quest

Mary the mother of Jesus has been the focus of an extraordinary amount of piety and theology down the centuries, and whatever it is she represents has been and remains central to the vitality of Christianity in many parts of the world. It would be worthwhile to try to understand that quite apart from the phenomenon of feminist theology. Mary is also, inevitably, a focus of discussion in inter-church dialogue—indeed, this particular discussion of my own had its origin in an invitation to me from the Oxford branch of the Ecumenical Society of the Blessed Virgin Mary, which requires of its members only that they should be prepared to say or sing the *Magnificat*, though it is a society unlikely to concern itself with feminism as a post-1960s movement, or with feminist theology. As an ecumenical society it will be unable to avoid that concern indefinitely, so long as women alert to feminist and feminist theological concerns continue to make the effort to participate in Christian institutional structures, or Christian societies. One recent attempt to contribute to ecumenical dialogue, with attention to women and their status in mind, is Pope John Paul II's Sixth Encyclical, *Redemptoris Mater* (Mother of the Redeemer) published on 25th March, 1987, to initiate the Marian year which began on Pentecost Sunday, 7th June, 1987, and which concluded on the Feast of Assumption, 15th August, 1988. The Feast, incidentally, survived the Reformation to remain in Oxford University's Calendar, though since it falls in the middle of the long vacation, it is not the focus or occasion of particular celebration, no doubt to the great relief of at least some of the Canons of Christ Church, at once college chapel and diocesan cathedral.

It may be helpful to make a statement about how this present writer sees the enterprise of feminist theology, before turning to my exploration of how Mary is now viewed by a variety of feminist and other theologians, moving along a spectrum from the extremely hostile to the more constructive— none of which falls along strictly denominational lines in any necessary way, so far as one can see. Feminist theologians within the Christian tradition have an argument with that tradition and its values for them in their present culture. If we agree to define feminism at its most minimal as a movement which seeks change for the better in terms of justice for women, it is obvious that a feminist theologian need not be female by sex; and not every female theologian is a feminist theologian.

The major feminist theologians at the present time are female, however, because a primary need for women is being expressed in this form of theology, that is, self-reliance in understanding themselves and their relationship to the God they have found to be theirs although mediated to them by a religious tradition which causes some of their problems. They are concerned to use gender analysis to examine the way religious traditions work, the symbolism they use, the characteristics of roles within them, the way religious traditions reflect social assumptions and shape and re-shape those assumptions, and especially the gender-related way in which we talk about divine reality. Theology is itself one such gender-related term, reflecting the unease about the association of the female and the feminine with the godlike. Feminist theologians hope that some of the old stories can be re-told and new ones invented to verbalise God in an inclusively human manner, which takes account of female human beings and what particular societies, including Christian ones, make of the biological differences which render some of us female and some of us male. The languages which mediate divine reality to us have differed depending on their relationship to shifting contexts, and feminist theologians want to imitate the motivation of those who have re-deployed the language, and perhaps even re use some of the content. The point of the whole endeavour is to try to get us to make an imaginative and moral shift, so that we can come to share a new vision of goodness and be given and gain access to it. This is hardly a destructive or unworthy goal, though the route there may be a painful one. For so far as feminist theologians are concerned, it is not just the biblical texts, but centuries of habits of exegesis, ecclesiastical practice and tradition which are now ripe for scrutiny, all alike without immunity of any kind. And this includes the texts and traditions and devotions about Mary.

Feminist theology is young, but women have been engaged in the re-evaluation of texts and traditions for some time. For instance, one Eliza Sharples in 1832 addressed a meeting, in the course of which she said:

> The tyrant God, Necessity, said to the subject man: 'Of the tree of knowledge of good and evil thou shalt not eat'. Sweet and fair Liberty stepped in spurned the order of the tyrant. 'She took of the fruit thereof, and did eat, and gave also unto her husband with her, and he did eat.' Do you not, with one voice exclaim, well done woman! LIBERTY FOR EVER! If that was a fall, sirs, it was a glorious fall, and such a fall as is now wanted ... I will be such an Eve, so bright a picture of liberty.[1]

And twelve years later, in 1844, reformer Emma Martin, who once lectured on 'The Holy Ghost, HER Nature, Offices and Laws' (presumably without the benefit of the Syrian Fathers) remarked 'I have asked the *learned(?)* clergy for rational answers to knotty questions ... they won't [sic] answer them because they are asked by a woman, yet they obtained Christ from the same source. I wonder they did not object to him on that account.'[2] The doyenne of the movement as a whole is Elizabeth Cady Stanton, veteran of the nineteenth century's anti-slavery campaign as well as of other battles, passionately concerned as she was about women's needs and their expression in society. In her eighties, she and a team of colleagues produced a collection of comments on the parts of the Bible which explicitly refer to women, published in 1895 and 1898 as *The Woman's Bible,* and in a new paperback edition in 1985.[3] It is convenient to pick up a passage from *The Woman's Bible,* which represents a not untypical reaction to the 1854 dogma. of the 'Immaculate Conception', a dogma not only profoundly troublesome to women, but also, given its long and contentious history, to the relationship between the Roman Catholic Church and other Churches, not just Protestant ones but Orthodox too. This will give us a line of connection to the present-day feminist critique. For the dogma states that:

> the Blessed Virgin Mary, in the first instant of her conception, has been, by a special grace and privilege of Almighty God, and in view of the merits of Jesus Christ, the Saviour of the human race, preserved and exempted from every stain of original sin.[4]

We could cite here as a commentary, as it were, *Redemptoris Mater:*

> In the liturgy the church salutes Mary of Nazareth as the church's own beginning, for in the event of the immaculate conception the church

sees projected and anticipated in her most noble member, the saving grace of Easter.[5]

In *The Woman's Bible* there is a comment from one of Elizabeth Cady Stanton's collaborators, which muddles two doctrines together, but nevertheless manages to make a point about the way in which this doctrine is still 'heard' and 'read' by women no matter what is said to them about what the doctrines are supposed to mean, that is, excluding women's meanings. Elizabeth Cady Stanton's collaborator seems to have written in some desperation from within a context of hopelessly idealised maternalism when she wrote that:

> I think that the doctrine of the Virgin birth as something higher, sweeter, nobler than ordinary motherhood, is a slur on all the natural motherhood of the world. I believe that millions of children have been as immaculately conceived, as purely born, as was the Nazarene. Why not? Out of this doctrine, and that which is akin to it, have sprung all the monasteries and nunneries of the world, which have disgraced and distorted and demoralised manhood and womanhood for a thousand years. I place beside the false, monkish, unnatural claim of the Immaculate Conception my mother, who was as holy in her motherhood as was Mary herself.[6]

Leaving aside for the moment the problems raised by Christian asceticism at its awful worst rather than at its splendid best, it is important to be honest about the way in which, as this writer has suggested, doctrines about Mary are consistently assessed by women (even when some kind of theoretical or doctrinal understanding seems to have been achieved) as suggesting the denigration of all other women who are mothers , or even just of all other women, mothers or not. As Edward Schillebeeckx so disastrously exclaimed, 'It is clear that she must be a creature of matchless wonder, this *Immaculat* and *Assumpta*, with whom even the most physically and spiritually beautiful women in the world cannot in any way be compared ...'[7]

Even without expressly defined dogma, in Orthodox tradition we may be invited to 'stand with reverence in the house of our God, and cry aloud: Hail, Queen of the world; hail, Mary, sovereign over all of us; hail, thou who alone art blameless and fair among women ...'[8] which may prompt a question about what all other women, as distinct from men, are being blamed for. Being first to sin could be part of the answer. And the *Te*

Deum sung at Anglican Matins includes as a reflection on the divine self-emptying, 'When thou tookest upon thee to deliver man / thou didst not abhor the Virgin's womb'. Why 'abhor'? Why should any woman's womb and body be thought of as a possible source of abhorrence? Quite apart from the astonishing prurience displayed in devotion to Mary on the part of some of her adherents,[9] not the least remarkable feature of the Christian tradition is the extreme rarity of the sane comment made by the ninth-century Ratramnus, attempting to combat beliefs consequent upon the assumption that the womb was impure, when he insisted firstly that no creature was created vile, and so, also, that 'a woman's uterus is not indecent, but honourable'.[10] He lost his argument.

Luther's attitude to women and to the feminine is somewhat complex, including what Jean Bethke Elshtain calls the 'institutional moment' of his masculinisation of theology—his assault on 'mother' church, and his loss of 'a female linked transcendent moment',[11] notwithstanding his personal devotion to Mary:

> She is my love, the noble Maid,
> Forget her can I never;
> Whatever honour men have paid,
> My heart she has for ever.[12]

To the present purpose what matters is his defence of the goodness of sexual desire, which led him to comment on Crotus, who

> wrote blasphemously about the marriage of priests, declaring that the most holy bishop of Mainz was irritated by no annoyance more than by the stinking, putrid, private parts of women. That godless knave, forgetful of his mother and sister, dares to blaspheme God's creature through whom he was himself born. It would be tolerable if he were to find fault with the behaviour of women, but to defile their creation and nature is most godless. As if I were to ridicule a man's face on account of his nose! For the nose is the latrine of man's head and stands above his mouth![13]

Not the most helpful analogy in the circumstances, but the general point stands. And for sheer punitive nastiness, there is little to beat the comment made by Suarez in 1584, who wrote of that 'troublesome weariness with which all pregnant women are burdened, she alone did not experience who alone conceived without pleasure'.[14] Another gem from the writings of a seventeenth-century male saint observes that, 'It is a subject of humiliation of all the mothers of children of Adam to know that while they are with child, they carry within them an infant who is the enemy of God, the object of his hatred and malediction and the shrine of the demon.'[15] This is at once a 'theological' response to the sheer difficulties of childbearing, from pregnancy, through birth to lactation and weaning, the risks to the mother, and to the high mortality rate common to children apart from those born in privileged societies, as well as being a preface to the assertion of the need for 're-birth' by baptism, normally male-administered.

What it may also express to women is the theology of 'God punished women more', which in the nineteenth and early twentieth centuries hindered the use of anaesthetic and analgesic drugs in childbirth even when these had become comparatively safe and available. Women were not seen as related to the new 'Eve', nor helped to experience birth as she may have done, relatively without pain and distress, a point made by Leonardo Boff, when he suggests that Mary was free not from pain itself, but from the way we have pain.[16]

If Elizabeth Cady Stanton is the doyenne of the nineteenth-century movement in feminist theology, Mary Daly is the doyenne of the twentieth-century one. Mary Daly indeed acknowledges that despite some elements of the tradition, Mary has been for many women their only symbol of hope, not least when they have been on what she calls 'spiritual starvation rations'[17]— which includes those of the Protestant tradition, eliminating not only Mary 'the apostle to the apostles', but Mary the mother of Jesus and such women saints as there were, from view. Before turning to Mary Daly's pungent comments on Mary the mother of Jesus, however, it is worth noticing that she is herself the product of the North American Roman Catholic tradition which by the time of the Second Vatican Council included some of the most formidably well-educated women in the USA. And to illuminate her exasperation with her original Communion, and that of other women with Christian institutions, we could refer to the documents of the Second Vatican Council,[18] and pay some attention to what they do and do not say about women, as about Mary, because apart from one or two distinctively Roman Catholic touches, the documents are not untypical of Christian attitudes to women.

The documents cut Mary down to size. In Leonardo Boff's book, *The Maternal Face of God*, he summarises various routes into Mariology, the second of which was the one followed by the Council. In the words of Boff's summary, 'Mary never lived in or for herself. Mary was a woman ever at the service of others—of God, of Christ, of redemption, of the Church, of the ultimate meaning of history.' From this perspective, Mary is never to be the subject of a theological consideration of her own, but finds her place in other theological treatises.[19] This feminine non-entity is purportedly rescued from redundancy by the claim that 'Our Lady is the creature who realised to a super-eminent degree whatever values are being discussed or mediated.' The language of perfection is thus largely transferred to the Church, a somewhat problematical move, but as Anne Carr comments in her book *Transforming Grace*,[20] Mary is still in contrast with 'Eve'—all other women—and it does not take much expertise to discover how they are to be viewed. In some respects, the documents of the Council are extremely promising. One of the few explicit references to women indeed regrets that fundamental personal rights are not universally honoured for women, such as the right and freedom to choose a husband, embrace a state of life, or acquire an education or cultural benefits equal to those recognised for men. And Pope Paul VI in International Women's Year in 1975 said that what is most urgent is 'to labour everywhere to have discovered, respected and protected the rights and prerogatives of every woman in her life—educational, professional, civic, social, religious—whether single or married'.[21] Paragraph 52 of 'The Church Today', on 'the nobility of marriage and the family', to its credit affirms that if the life of the family is to flower it needs kindly communion of minds and painstaking co-operation of the parents in the education of their children. But there is no sense that things could be different and indeed better in what follows:

> The active presence of the father is highly beneficial to their formation. The children, especially the younger among them, need the care of their mother at home. This domestic role of *hers* [my emphasis] must be safely preserved, though the legitimate social progress of women should not be underrated on that account.

What the writers miss is the essential active presence of a father to his children, not least to his daughter(s), and the effects on women of their continued restriction to the 'private', as distinct from the public and political realms, reinforced by suburban housing patterns; not to mention the massive double work burden many of them carry for a very long time, inside their homes in 'unpaid' work, and outside their homes in paid employment, necessary if their families are not to fall into poverty. And in societies where the family is still the economic unit, some fifty percent of the Third World's food is produced by women, including their work at the heavy agricultural labour involved. How then are women to read not only the documents of the Council, but the words of *Redemptoris Mater*?

> In the light of Mary, the church sees in the face of women the reflection
> of a beauty which mirrors the loftiest sentiments of which the human
> heart is capable: the self-offering totality of love; the strength that is
> capable of bearing the greatest sorrows; limitless fidelity and tireless
> devotion to work; the ability to combine penetrating intuition with
> words of support and encouragement.

Women's well-being may well depend upon their finding at least some of
these characteristics less than unambiguously praiseworthy.

In Section 60 of the Council's assessment of 'The Church Today', it is
indeed acknowledged that women are now employed in almost every area
of life, so that it is deemed appropriate 'that they should be able to assume
their full proper role *in accordance with their own nature*' (my emphasis).
Given the peculiar association of women, rather than men, with nature,
it seems to be understood that women's nature is both well-defined and
limiting, though there is an implicit concession to new possibilities in the
need for everyone to 'acknowledge and favour the proper and necessary
participation of women in cultural life', and other options seem to be
indicated in the sentence added during the final drafting to paragraph 9
of the document on the laity, in the section on 'the various fields of the
apostolate', pointing out the importance of women's participation in the
various fields of the Church's apostolate. Readers are no doubt meant to
be reassured by the footnote which draws attention to the point that this is
one of the few places in all the council documents where special attention
is given to the contribution of women to the mission of the Church, though
it was clearly (to whom?) the mind of the Council that they were included
'and eminently so', whenever the general role of the laity was discussed. The
note adds that by the time the Council ended, twelve lay and ten 'religious'
women were present as 'auditrices', though not of course what Anne Carr
records, that no woman was allowed to read a paper before the assembly
(cf. 1 Timothy 2:12, presumably), and that attempts were made to try to bar
women journalists from attending council masses or receiving communion
during its meetings.[22] Real exasperation could be provoked by the closing
messages of the Council, messages to men (males) regarded in terms of
their diversified contributions to society, with women having a message
addressed to them alone, and as is typical in Christianity, with reference
to their sexual states.[23] Women are addressed as girls, wives, mothers and
widows, as consecrated virgins, and women living alone, though with the
acknowledgment that they constitute half of the immense human family,

and with the claim that the Church has 'glorified and liberated' them, a claim not without weight, notwithstanding this present reading of the Council's documents. Women are associated with 'the protection of the home', with cradles and deaths (cf. the nativity and crucifixion scenes?). Mothers are exhorted to 'pass on to your sons and daughters the traditions of your fathers'—mothers not having any? Women are invited to reconcile men with life, to guard purity, unselfishness and piety, to aid men to retain courage in *their* great undertakings, with women's own concern to be particularly with the peace of the world. They are clearly excluded from the address to 'workers'—'very loved sons', with its sense of unease, mistrust and lack of understanding between the institution and the workers.

It was in response to the Council that one of the most important books in feminist theology appeared in 1968, Mary Daly's *The Church and the Second Sex*, and the invitation to write that book was prompted by an article of hers which was published in 1965 when she already had a doctorate in theology from Fribourg University in Switzerland, where she was studying philosophy. Mary Daly and Rosemary Radford Ruether were crucial in forming the women's caucus within the American Academy of Religion, at which they both delivered important papers in 1971. Rosemary Radford Ruether's was to appear as 'Misogynism and virginal feminism in the fathers of the church', available with other useful essays in the collection she edited called *Religion and Sexism: Images of Women in the Jewish and Christian Traditions* (1974).[24] Mary Daly's much reprinted essay had a deliberately menacing title: 'Theology after the demise of God the Father; a call for the castration of sexist religion', and she was to part company with Christianity in the course of writing *Beyond God the Father* (1973), re-issued with an 'Original Reintroduction'. One also needs to read *Gyn/Ecology* (1978)[25] and *Pure Lust* (1984),[26] each of which contains devastating attacks on Christianity's core symbolism. Tucked away in a footnote of *Beyond God the Father* is her assessment of Phyllis Trible's paper of 1973 on 'Depatriarchalizing in Biblical Tradition', on which Mary Daly commented that 'It might be interesting to speculate upon the probable length of a "depatriarchalized Bible". Perhaps there would be enough salvageable material to comprise an interesting pamphlet'.[27] It is relevant to bear this in mind particularly when we attend to her treatment of the story of the Annunciation.

For Mary Daly, Mary is killed by the dogmas about her, killed, though apparently alive, like a dolled-up Christmas tree. She points out that the 1854 definition (which was in the forefront of the attention of Elizabeth

Cady Stanton's collaborator's mind) coincides with the first wave of feminism, though it is in fact doubtful that the definition was aimed at feminism. Here is a woman preserved from original sin by the grace of her son not only in advance of his birth but of her own. As *Redemptoris Mater* puts it, 'together with the Father, the Son has chosen her, entrusting her eternally to the Spirit of holiness …'. What she is purified from is her own autonomous being; her psyche is already dismembered; and the story of the Annunciation affirming her need of male acceptance—'according to thy will'—makes her doubly a victim. She can then function only as a token woman of hope, since she stands over against the incompetence and array of weaknesses ascribed to women in general. So for Mary Daly, the impossible ideal of Virgin/Mother has ultimately a punitive function, since no actual woman can live up to it, throwing all women back into the status of the 'first Eve, and essentially reinforcing the universality of women's low-caste status'.[28] Yet she acknowledges that the Immaculate Conception could be understood as the negation of the myth of feminine evil, foreshadowing the 'Fall into the sacred… free from the crippling burden of submersion in the role of the Other'.[29]

This is the convenient point to couple with her opinions of the 1854 dogma Mary Daly's treatment of the 1950 dogma of the Assumption: 'The Immaculate Mother of God, Mary ever virgin, having run the course of her earthly life, was taken up body and soul into the glory of heaven …'. Edward Yarnold, SJ, has eloquently pointed out the differences, let us say, between the Assumption as painted by Titian and an icon of the Dormition in the Orthodox tradition, maintaining nonetheless that 'Both sides of Christendom believe that Mary was received body and soul into heaven to be reunited with her Son in glory'.[30] Mary Daly has made the point that the dogma could at long last indicate a 'no' to the peculiar association of women with sin and flesh and matter, and it could also, in the immediate post-World War II period, remind us of the importance of bodies, even indeed of Jewish ones. Unfortunately, the dogma's promulgation coincided with a backlash against female independence, not wholly understandable as part of the need to re-found families. For Mary Daly, this dogma then annihilates women's earthly presence, and rehabilitates her as defeated, eliminated from public life, saved, once again, by the male.[31] Given her assessment of the male monogender mating of the Trinity, one could see too what she might make of Leonardo Boff's attempts to secure a special relation of the third 'person' of the Trinity with Mary, Boff breaking well out of the constrictions of the Vatican II documents.

Salvation for women by a God manifested contingently as a male was coped with in earlier periods via the analogy of 'male is to female as form is to matter', an analogy no longer defensible, any more than is an assumption associated with it, that 'the first and principal cause of offspring is always in the father', and here Marina Warner's book on Mary is illuminating. She quotes the passage in Aeschylus' *Oresteia*, where Orestes at his trial cries out in protest, 'And dost thou call me a blood relation of my mother?' Apollo arbitrates with the judgment that 'The so-called offspring is not produced by the mother ... She is not more than the nurse, as it were, of the newly conceived foetus. It is the male who is the author of its being'.[32] This has been untenable without considerable qualification since the development of embryology from the early nineteenth century onwards (and Boff, to his credit, tries to pay attention to this development), but it still influences doctrines about the ministry as it does doctrines about Mary. So in the Bishop of London's November 1985 newsletter he did his best to elaborate the view that 'in the whole of human instinct and understanding it is the masculine which is associated with giving and the feminine with receiving', a piece of gender construction as intolerable for men as it is dishonest about women, and in the latter is liable to produce some hilarity in those who have become aware of and articulate about their role in securing the well-being of men without any firm expectation that the converse will obtain. In Marian doctrines, we can still see the influence of this theory, which has to do with what a culture thinks reproduction is all about, that is 'the relationship between procreative beliefs and the wider context (world view, cosmology, culture) in which they are found'.[33] Paternity, in Carol Delaney's analysis, has meant 'the primary, essential and creative role' in reproduction, and the meaning of maternity as 'nurture' is epitomised by Mary.

Carol Delaney takes the root meaning of 'virgin birth' (and we may add the dogmas already mentioned) to be a version of *folk* theories about procreation, the essential implication of which is that a child originates from only one source, and so is entirely consistent with theological monotheism. Her fieldwork in a Turkish Muslim village enabled her to identify an appropriate theory of procreation, which is that 'The male is said to plant the seed and the woman is said to be like a field', so the woman's role is secondary, supportive and nurturant. So she identifies a further analogy, of 'Woman is to Man as the created, natural world is to God', and we connect this again with metaphors from the Orthodox liturgy quoted earlier. First:

Then the power of the Most High overshadowed her that knew not
wedlock, so that she might conceive: and he made her fruitful womb
as a fertile field for all who long to reap the harvest of salvation,
singing: Alleluia![34]

Second, we find Mary urged by the unborn John in Elizabeth's womb to
rejoice as the 'vine with unwithering shoot', 'farm with untainted fruit',
'arable yielding a bountiful stack of pity', 'furbishing a lush pasturage'.[35]

Carol Delaney is surely correct to point out that the knowledge that
women are co-engenderers, co-creators, providing half the 'seed' so to
speak, half the genetic constitution of the child in addition to pregnancy,
birth and suckling, has not yet been encompassed symbolically. Paternity is
indeed a cultural construction of a powerful kind, and one cannot simply
claim that the meaning of Mary's virginity is that 'the role played by the
human race in the Incarnation is simply that of accepting God's gift as a
gift and as a grace, and nothing more',[36] yet another gender construction
associating receptivity with the feminine and giving with the masculine.
Though there is something important to hold on to here for our culture, as
Lochman wrote in his comment on how Mr Fix-It is set aside, for humanity
in the Incarnation is involved 'in the form not of a primarily creating,
controlling, self-assertive, self-glorifying humanity but as a primarily
listening, receiving, serving and blessed ("graced") human being', as Mary
is impressively described in the Christmas narrative.[37] *Redemptoris Mater*,
however, returns us firmly to gender construction, influenced apparently
by a particular school of psychology, when the text says that in Mary's faith,
first at the annunciation and then fully at the foot of the cross, 'an interior
space was reopened within humanity which the eternal Father can fill "with
every spiritual blessing"...'.

One needs also to look at another strand in the tradition, which has to
do with the point that early Christianity offered women who did not or
could not fulfil certain socio-sexual roles a new kind of aspiration,[38] and for
them, the virgin Mary was a possible symbol of that discipleship which took
overriding priority in their lives. For to be sexually virginal was to be freed
from a measure of male domination, to be unexploited and unexploitable,
to enjoy a certain sense of transcendence as an element of personhood,
so sexual asceticism was not necessarily imposed on women as a kind of
constraint. This is an important and neglected possibility in the Protestant
tradition. Even Mary Daly acknowledges this, when she writes that the
doctrine that Mary was a virgin before, during and after the birth of Jesus,

'by its very absurdity… literally screams that biology and abstinence from sexual activity are not the essential dimensions of the symbol of Mary as a virgin…'.[39] The doctrine may be saying something about female autonomy to women, about the possibility of women's relation to divine reality without male mediation, although there is a further problem about the metaphors used to indicate the divine that would have to be tackled at this as at other points of Christian doctrine. And Mary Daly and others may be mistaken about the possibility of enjoying transcendence and autonomy without the necessity for sexual virginity or chastity, depending on how sexual relationships are construed and function in a particular society. Sarah Maitland's brilliant novel *Daughter of Jerusalem* (1978) catches this element of virginity beautifully in her initial reflection on Mary, small, dark, devout, probably illiterate, unconventional, of unassailable self-assurance:

> Of course her assent is a sexual act, she tried to explain, pushing her hair back under her scarf, and grinding her bare toes into the coarse sand, because it was complete, it was made with the whole of her being. It was an assent to the totality of herself, to a womanhood so vital and empowered that it could break free of biology and *submission*, any dependence on or need for a masculine sexuality—that furrow in which the crop of women's sex has been held to be rooted.[40]

One extremely important manifestation of this sense of 'womanhood' was that it made the pursuit of learning possible, even if it often meant retreat from the public world into the seclusion of the book-lined cell—not the worst of all fates. Helen Waddell might be approximately a good twentieth-century example, daughter of an Irish Presbyterian missionary family as she was, even though reading the sympathetic biography of her by Dame Felicitas Corrigan may still leave one with a sense of regret for a life not entirely fulfilled. But consider, for example, what is expressed in her translation of a ninth-century lament for a young abbess, a translation made during the bombing raids of September 1941, which makes it all the more poignant:

> Thou hast come safe to port,
> I still at sea,
> The light is on thy head,
> Darkness in me.
> Pluck thou in heaven's field
> Violet and rose

> Whilst I strew flowers that will thy vigil keep,
> Where thou dost sleep,
> Love, in thy last repose.[41]

And we could add to that her translation of an eleventh-century verse about the virgins in the fields of the blessed, the girls illustrated as it were in Fra Angelico's picture of St Thomas Aquinas and St Bonaventura conversing in Paradise together:

> Gertrude, Agnes, Prisca, Cecily,
> Lucia, Thekla, Petronel,
> Agatha, Barbara, Juliana,
> Wandering there in the fresh spring meadows,
> Looking for flowers to make them a garland,
> Roses red of the Passion,
> Lilies and violets for love.[42]

We have forgotten why it was that virginity could signal a vocation, and this forgetfulness has in part to do with its praise by undoubted woman-haters, even making the most generous allowances in the interpretation of the rhetoric of misogyny. For virginity may be associated also with stony *a*sexuality, and the bizarre behaviour which can accompany it, the product of a tradition which deemed women not to be as godlike as men are, approximating to godlikeness only in so far as they approximate to masculinity. When males are taken to be the normative and representative and essentially life-giving expression of the human species, with females as defective, imperfect and merely nurturant human beings, then virginity changes its meaning, and signifies the approximation to an ideal one can never reach. One manifestation of this is the phenomenon of anorexia, the inability to eat, not necessarily a religious or indeed peculiarly Christian phenomenon, but undoubtedly present in those women with a passion for what they took to be moral and spiritual perfection—virility and virtue—an approximation to that image of deity they might be thought not to bear in their own right. The asceticism necessary for the pursuit of their virginal vocation sometimes tipped them into uncontrollable anorexia and so to amenorrhea, not least where they were in rebellion against the dependent forms of Christianity on offer to women. Getting control of her body in asceticism however extreme, retrieves a woman from the sense of helplessness she experiences simply by virtue of being female. It commands attention, and for a time, tremendous energy, as well as the ability to by-pass religious controls, find communion with the deity, and criticise popes and archbishops.

The search for transcendence here can tip women into near or actual half-unconscious destruction as petrified living dead.[43] If, however, we could retrieve the association of 'virgin' with autonomy, but carefully balanced with a sense of co-inherence, and without the abasement of a woman's visual image;[44] and if we could by-pass sugary sweetness and dizzy immobilisation on a pedestal, then Mary might be re-associated with the affirmation and not the negation of what women discover themselves to be, and we might re-connect Mary to present needs as, for example, Rosemary Radford Ruether attempts to do.[45]

She, like Mary Daly, wants female presence acknowledged without fear of real women, a fear not always unjustifiable; she wants the co-ordination of nature and grace recovered for those whose ecclesiastical traditions have lost it—again, arguably expressed in Mary's rapturous assent. Arguing that we cannot remain with a doctrine of salvation mediated by the male alone, she asks for the genuine reciprocity of women and men together in the Churches, an expression of the way in which the female plays a co-operating role in the work of salvation. This could have important consequences outside the Church too, in the support each person gives to the dignity and self-actualisation of the other. We could connect with this ideal of 'reciprocity', a remark of C. S. Lewis'—astonishingly, since he is not frequently associated with perceptive comments about the reciprocity of men and women together, of a kind which women can recognise as being supportive to them. Yet perhaps as a result of his life with Joy Davidman he was to write after her death:

> It is arrogance in us to call frankness, fairness and chivalry 'masculine' when we see them in a woman; it is arrogance in them to describe a man's sensitiveness or tact or tenderness as 'feminine'. But also what poor, warped fragments of humanity most mere men and mere women must be to make the implications of that arrogance plausible.[46]

And it is Lewis, too, who anticipated in a way the appropriation of Mary for 'liberation' theology, writing of Jesus as very much his mother's son, in his *Reflections on the Psalms*:

> There is a fierceness, even a touch of Deborah, mixed with the sweetness in the *Magnificat* to which most painted Madonnas do little justice; matching the frequent severity of His own sayings. I am

sure that the private life of the holy family was, in many senses, 'mild' and 'gentle', but perhaps hardly in the way some hymn writers have in mind. One may suspect, on proper occasions, a certain astringency; and all in what people at Jerusalem regarded as a rough north-country accent.[47]

Rosemary Radford Ruether ties the *Magnificat* in to the revolutionary spirit of liberation theology (a possibility obliterated for centuries by the practice of having it sung by pre-pubescent boys in skirts and frills) with women above all representing the 'nobodies' made to be persons as a result of the self-emptying of divine power in Jesus. Anne Carr makes Mary herself a symbol of the transformed world for which women hope, edging away from Mary as the impossible double-bind figure identified by Mary Daly. Anne Carr acknowledges that Mary is a utopian figure, a mystery. 'Her intimate place in the Christian pattern enables us to imagine a healed, reconciled, finally transformed world. While it is God who works human salvation in Christ, and the Spirit who inspires the active response of the Church, it is Mary who is the sign of the final transformation of the world.'[48]

There remain, however, a number of less 'orthodox' possibilities. Marina Warner[49] and Mary Daly[50] both spot something else in Mary which makes her important to women exhausted by imperceptive moralism, and this was something explained, oddly enough, in *The Times* of 7 February, 1987, by Rabbi Ephraim Gastwirth, though he evidently disapproves of what he describes, preferring, rather, 'the love and fear of a stern father'. For mother, he tells us, has a love which is eternal, and her broad arms encompass all her children without distinction. 'Indeed, her love is often stronger for the weak and wayward child, seeking to ensure his survival and to keep him within the family group. The mother's love is unconditional.' The point is that there is a sense in which Mary is as splendidly unconventional as Jesus was, since her loyalty to her own explodes the bounds of strict justice, as Marina Warner makes clear. 'Through her, the whole gay crew of wanton, loving, weak humanity finds its way to paradise'. So Marina Warner quotes the devils who say, 'Heaven's the place for all the riff-raff / We've got the wheat and God the chaff.'[51] This association of Mary with unconventional love and with self-determination, could relate her back to some less hallowed women, taking a clue from the genealogy of the First Gospel— women such as Ruth, Tamar, Rahab and Bathsheba, all specially related to messianic promise,[52] as well as to some of the thoroughly idiosyncratic women of the apostolic tradition. We would recall that Elizabeth's greeting,

'Blessed art thou among women', recalls comparable blessings to both Jael and Judith, before paying close attention also to the woman who wiped Jesus' feet with her hair, to the Syro-Phoenician woman who argues it out with him as does Martha in the Fourth Gospel, the Samaritan woman of the same Gospel, first missionary despite her past, and Mary of Magdala, not that figment of ecclesiastical imagination, a reformed prostitute, but someone healed of 'demonic' illness by Jesus. This 'apostle to the apostles' proclaims the resurrection as did the mother of the Maccabean martyrs, and is followed by Phoebe the deacon, Junia, given apostolic acknowledgment by Paul, and many others. And Elisabeth Moltmann-Wendel has made a particularly interesting reassessment of tradition about Mary,[53] pleading for much more honesty about its biblical origins, with the limitations imposed by that origin, and makes us see Mary as a 'living, critical, angry unadapted mother', just as difficult as some of the other people around Jesus, men as well as women. She emphasises that Mary needs to take her place, perhaps a pre eminent place, but only one place, among all these other 'sisters'. Elisabeth Moltmann-Wendel suggests that one of the greatest defects of the tradition, even with the presence of at least some women saints available, has been its monolithic character, the attempt to load into just one symbol much of what women can represent in human life, to men primarily, but with women finding in Mary possibilities for themselves. Feminist theologians who follow Elisabeth Moltmann-Wendel's lead will not want Mary confined by ecclesiastical definition however subtle, but want to be able to relate Mary to other women and the multiplicity of vocations and possibilities of their lives now and in the future. So if, and only if, women want to find role models in biblical and non-biblical tradition, Mary may still have something to offer.

Elisabeth Moltmann-Wendel made a proposal, 'Becoming human in new community', at the World Council of Churches meeting in Sheffield, in June 1981, 'The community of women and men in the Church', the proceedings of which were edited by Constance Parvey.[54] In her report on the meeting, Constance Parvey drew special attention to the fact that Mary had been singled out as one of the basic paradigms, not least in the section on tradition and traditions. She wrote that Mary is seen as a sharing woman seeking out Elizabeth to tell the news of her pregnancy; as being in the tradition of prophecy; neglected by her son in favour of his mission; and as a disciple journeying in partnership with Jesus along with other women and men. 'Then we witness her profound grief at the death of her child under the judgement of religious and political powers, her faithfulness to follow him to the tomb, and the divine gift bestowed upon her to be a witness of the resurrection of the "flesh of her flesh, the bone of her bone". Here is no model of submission and subordination, but someone fully living out her partnership with God in the Christ event.[55]

Between the present and the fulfilment of Anne Carr's vision, there are elements here which could be extremely valuable to those who still find their resources in the Christian tradition in relation to the appalling circumstances of their lives, as well as in hope for blessing and flourishing.

This essay represents a stage in exploration and does not attempt to do more than indicate some options. For the present writer, the least that could be said about Mary is that she represents what novelist Robertson Davies suggests in his phrase 'having the body in the soul's keeping',[56] but also, that 'Grace is not faceless', to quote Cornelius Ernst OP.[57] The material drawn on towards the end of the essay, however, would edge us towards meaning for that phrase rather more incarnated in women's lives than theology has so far been prepared to concede.

NOTES TO CHAPTER 1

[1] Quoted in Barbara Taylor, *Eve and the New Jerusalem: Socialism and Feminism in the Nineteenth Century* (London: Virago, 1983), p.146.

[2] Taylor, *Eve and the New Jerusalem*, p. 153.

[3] Elizabeth Cady Stanton, *The Women's Bible* (Edinburgh: Polygon, 1985).

[4] Cited from Karl Rahner, *Theological Investig*ations (London: Darton, Longman and Todd, 1961), Vol. 1, p. 201.

[5] *Redemptoris Mater*, as published in *Origins: NC Documentary Service*, Vol. 16.43 (9 April, 1987), pp. 745-67.

[6] Cady Stanton, *Women's Bible*, p. 114.

[7] Edward Schillebeeckx, *Mary, Mother of the Redemption* (London: Sheed and Ward, 1964), p. 172.

[8] Ecumenical Society of the Blessed Virgin Mary [ESBVM], *The Akathistos Hymn* (Oxford: Bocardo Press, 1987), p. 17.

[9] Hilda Graef, *Mary: A History of Doctrine and Devotion* (London: Sheed and Ward, 1985), p. 245, quoting from the twelfth-century Amadeus of Lausanne: 'The Holy Spirit will come upon you, that at this touch your womb may tremble and swell, your spirit rejoice and your womb flower ...'.

[10] Graef, *History of Doctrine and Devotion*, p. 176.

[11] Jean Bethke Elshtain, 'Luther *Sic*—Luther *Non*', *Theology Today* 63 (1986): 155-68, at pp. 167-8. And see chapter two of her *Meditations on Modern Political Thought: Masculine/Feminine Themes from Luther to Arendt* (New York, N.Y.: Praeger, 1986).

[12] Vincent White, *Soul and Psyche: An Enquiry into the Relationship of Psychotherapy and Religion* (London: Collins, 1969), p. 134, quoting the translation of another Dominican, Sebastian Bullough. And see Max Thurian, *Mary, Mother of the Lord, Figure of the Church* (London: Mowbray, 1985/1963) for more material on the Marian theology and devotion of the Reformers.

[13] Jean Bethke Elshtain, *Public Man, Private Woman* (Oxford: Robertson, 1981), p. 87.

[14] Marina Warner, *Alone of All Her Sex* (London: Picador, 1985), p. 43.

[15] Warner, *Alone of All Her Sex*, p. 57.

[16] Leonardo Boff, *The Maternal Face of God* (San Francisco, Cal.: Harper and Row, 1987/1979), p. 148.

[17] Mary Daly, *Beyond God the Father* (London: Women's Press, 1986/1973), p. 81f.

[18] Walter M. Abbot, ed., *The Documents of Vatican II* (London: Chapman, 1965).

[19] Boff, *Maternal Face*, pp. 10f.

[20] Anne Carr, *Transforming Grace: Christian Tradition and Women's Experience* (San Francisco, Cal.: Harper and Row, 1988), p. 191.

[21] Carr, *Transforming Grace*, p. 33.

[22] Carr, *Transforming Grace*, p. 30.

[23] Abbot, ed., *Documents*, pp. 732-5.

[24] Rosemary Radford Ruether, ed., *Religion and Sexism: Images of Women in the Jewish and Christian Traditions* (New York, N.Y.: Simon and Shuster, 1974).

[25] Mary Daly, *Gyn/Ecology* (London: Women's Press, 1984).

[26] Mary Daly, *Pure Lust* (London: Women's Press, 1984).

[27] Daly, *Beyond God the Father*, p. 205.

[28] Daly, *Beyond God the Father*, p. 81f.

[29] Daly, *Beyond God the Father*, p. 86.

[30] Edward Y. Yarnold, 'The Assumption', 1980 Assumption Day Lecture for the Parish Church of St Mary and All Saints, Walsingham.

[31] Daly, *Pure Lust*, p. 128.

[32] Warner, *Alone of All Her Sex*, p. 41.

[33] Carol Delaney, 'The Meaning of Paternity and the Virgin Birth Debate', *Man* 21 (1986): 454-513.

[34] ESBVM, *Akathistos Hymn*, p. 19.

[35] ESBVM, *Akathistos Hymn*, p. 33.

[36] John McHugh, 'The Virginal Conception of Jesus', paper of 25th October, 1985, published for the ESBVM, p. 6.

[37] Jan Milic Lochman, *The Faith We Confess: An Ecumenical Dogmatics* (Philadelphia, Penn.: Fortress Press, 1984), pp. 112-13.

[38] Ross S. Kraemer, 'The Conversion of Women to Ascetic Forms of Christianity', *Signs* 6 (1980): 298-307.

[39] Daly, *Beyond God the Father*, p. 85.

[40] Sara Maitland, *Daughters of Jerusalem* (London: Pavanne, 1987), p. 30.

[41] Dame Feliticas Corrigan, *Helen Waddell: A Biography* (London: Gollancz, 1986), p. 317.

[42] Helen Waddell, *The Wandering Scholars* (Harmondsworth: Penguin, 1954), p. 123.

[43] See Chapter 3 of Ann Loades, *Searching for Lost Coins: Explorations in Christianity and Feminism* (London: SPCK, 1987).

[44] Ruether, *Religion and Sexism*, p. 166.

[45] Rosemary Radford Ruether, *Mary, the Feminine Face of the Church* (London: SCM Press, 1979) and Chapter 6 of her *Sexism and God-talk: Towards a Feminist Theology* (London: SCM Press, 1983).

[46] C. S. Lewis, *A Grief Observed* (London: Faber, 1986), p. 43.

[47] C. S. Lewis, *Reflections on the Psalms* (London: Fontana, 1961), p. 13.

[48] Carr, *Transforming Grace*, p. 193.

[49] Warner, *Alone of All Her Sex*, and its chapter on 'The Hour of Our Death'.

[50] Daly, *Beyond God the Father*, pp. 91-2.

[51] Warner, *Alone of All Her Sex*, p. 325.

[52] Raymond E. Brown. Karl P. Donfield, Joseph A. Fitzmyer and John Reumann, eds, *Mary in the New Testament* (London: Chapman, 1978), p. 82; cf. Janice Capel Anderson, 'Mary's Difference: Gender and Patriarchy in the Birth Narratives', *Journal of Religion* 97 (1987): 183-202.

[53] Elisabeth Moltmann-Wendell, *A Land Flowing With Milk and Honey* (London: SCM Press, 1986), p. 193f.

[54] Constance Parvey, ed., *The Community of Women and Men in the Church: A Report of the World Council of Churches' Conference, Sheffield, England, 1981* (Geneva: WCC, 1983); cf. *The Ecumenical Review* Vol. 110.1 (January 1988), for articles developing the community study.

[55] Parvey, ed., *Community of Women and Men*, p. 141.

[56] Robertson Davies, *The Rebel Angels* (Harmondsworth: Penguin, 1985), p. 56.

[57] Cornelius Ernst, *Multiple Echo* (London: Darton, Longman and Todd, 1979), p. 124. Patricia and Charles Vereker gave me hospitality when I wrote the first draft of this paper. I am immensely grateful to them , and to audiences in Oxford, Earlham College , Richmond, Indiana, Vanderbilt Divinity School, and especially the Faculties of the Lutheran School of Divinity, Chicago, and Catholic Theological Union, Chicago, for their comments. Professor Herbert Anderson arranged for me to read this paper at CTU, at which I had the privilege of meeting Professor Anne Carr, Professor Dianne Bergant and Professor Carolyn Osiek. Without the hospitality Professors Herbert and Phyllis Anderson gave me whilst in Chicago, this paper would not have developed as it has, and my final thanks are specially to them.

2

Mary: For Everyone

It seems to me that Mary is a significant symbol in the ecumenical context.[1] This is for the simple reason that whatever it is that is symbolized by her has been and remains central to the vitality of Christianity in many parts of the world, though some are still vigorous in their protest that this is the case.[2] A relatively new feature of ecumenical dialogue, however, is the contribution made by women to it, and some of them are alert to feminist theological concerns. So long as these women continue to make the effort to participate in Christian institutions or societies, their voices are bound, one hopes, to make a difference to the way theology is done, and how it comes out. And it can require a considerable effort to stay, in the face of reproaches that one is betraying other women and their needs by so doing, since there exists some justifiable criticism of what the Christian tradition has had and still does have on offer for women.

Much depends on whether one thinks that a tradition is or can be alive enough to change for the better—it is not change just for the sake of it. And there are signs of hope, as for instance in *Marialis Cultus (To Honour Mary)* of 1974. So, in paragraph 34 Pope Paul VI maintains:

> Devotion to the Blessed Virgin must also pay close attention to certain findings of the human sciences. This will help to eliminate one of the causes of the difficulties experienced in devotion to the Mother of the Lord, namely, the discrepancy existing between some aspects of this devotion and modem anthropological discoveries and the profound changes which have occurred in the psycho-sociological field in which modem man lives and works. The picture of the Blessed Virgin presented in a certain type of devotional literature cannot easily be reconciled with today's life style, especially with the way women live

today. In the home, women's equality and coresponsibility with man in the running of the family are being justly recognized by laws and the evolution of customs. In the sphere of politics women have in many countries gained a position in public life equal to that of men. In the social field women are at work in a whole range of different employments, getting further away every day from the restricted surroundings of the home. In the cultural field new possibilities are opening up for women in scientific research and intellectual activities.

In some ways, one might say that the papal sketch needs to be more sharply drawn. For instance, it needs to advert clearly to the massive double work burden most women have always carried, inside their homes in 'unpaid' work and outside their homes in paid employment, necessary if their families are not to fall into poverty. In societies where the family is still the economic unit, at least half of the so-called Third World's food is produced by women, including their work at the heavy agricultural labour involved. In so-called First-World cultures women can suffer in different ways if restricted to the 'private' as distinct from the public and political realms, reinforced by suburban housing patterns; and, as we know, home can be hell for other reasons. What could the symbolization of Mary have to do with all this? Not simply, one hopes, what another papal document *Redemptoris Mater (Mother of the Redeemer)* calls 'limitless fidelity and tireless devotion to work',[3] since these are not unambiguously praiseworthy qualities in many contexts.

Marialis Cultus goes on to point up Mary as a disciple (para 35) which in the Gospels at least (as distinct from other parts of the New Testament) even for women has little to do with domesticity. The women associated with Jesus of Nazareth are an unconventional group, to put it mildly. Paragraph 36 of *Marialis Cultus* also comments that:

> It should be considered quite normal for succeeding generations of Christians in differing socio-cultural contexts to have expressed their sentiments about the Mother of Jesus in a way and manner which reflected their own age.

And further:

> When the Church considers the long history of Marian devotion she rejoices at the continuity of the element of cult which it shows, but she does not bind herself to any particular expression of an individual cultural epoch or to the particular anthropological ideas underlying

such expressions. The Church understands that certain outward religious expressions, while perfectly valid in themselves, may be less suitable to men and women of different ages and cultures.

Various scriptural reflections follow, which offer us a Mary taken into dialogue with God, giving her active and responsible consent to what was to happen, a woman of courageous choice, a woman who proclaims God's vindication of those who need it, who survived poverty, flight and exile, who presumably brought her family through it, but was far from being exclusively concerned with her own family (any more than were other women in the Gospels, we might add).

We need not minimize the difficulties men as well as women may have with traditions about Mary. For instance, *Under the Heel of Mary*[4] is a fascinating but sorry story about Marianism, which includes reference to Mary as 'exterminator of all heresies', as a symbol for cold war warriors and for some of those who promoted the dogma of the Assumption, as well as 'Our Lady of National Security'. And Mary of the *Magnificat* may be an uncomfortable figure of a different kind for a church producing an indigenous theology in South America (liberation theology), requiring primarily liberation from the thugs and torturers of that continent, but also from possibly inappropriate hierarchical structures in the Church itself. For women, in the first instance, but also for men, if we are to be serious about humanly inclusive theology, we need to think about feminist theology and Mary as a significant figure in the tradition. As it happens, the 1986 conference of the Ecumenical Society of the Blessed Virgin Mary included one from Donal Flanagan,[5] 'Mary: some problems in ambivalence' which he concluded by asking: 'Are we then doomed to choose between an ecclesiastical Mary unrelated to twentieth-century woman and a theory of woman, feminism, which has no place for the greatest woman who ever lived?' He held out the possibility that 'these rock-hard certainties which now clash so destructively will slowly mature towards a constructive ambivalence and through that stage to a new vision'. We may now have arrived at that stage of 'constructive ambivalence', with even some elements of the new vision in the sightlines, which is what feminist theology in the end is all about, assuming that to be feminist and to be a feminist theologian is not a contradiction in terms, of course.

One fundamental problem highlighted by feminist theology is the gap between the *proclamation* of full personhood for women (associated in some parts of the tradition with the 'new Eve-Mary') and the *practice* of associating them with the 'old Eve'. On the one hand, male-and-female together 'image' God (Gen. 1); and Galatians signals that in the Christian community one abandons supposed privileges of race, social status and sex. Some of this has been conveyed by the symbol of Mary as a symbol of honour for women, not just for Mary, in the sense that honour for one is honour for all those like her. A woman who will quiz an archangel, give her (rapturous? enthusiastic?) assent, or agreement to the divine spirit working within her, risk scandal and single parenthood is, one might think, something of a risk-taker, and by no means a model of submission, subordination and passivity. To hail her (in Traherne's version, in the Ecumenical Office of the Ecumenical Society of the Blessed Virgin Mary) as 'Daughter of the Eternal Father, Mother of the Eternal Son, Spouse of the Eternal Spirit, Tabernacle of the most glorious Trinity' is at one level absurdly extravagant, but in so far as women have been allied with her, Mary is thus symbol of affirmation for them. Even so hostile a critic of the tradition as Mary Daly acknowledges that very problematical dogmas, such as the Immaculate Conception, can signal to women the negation of the myth of feminine evil, that is, the association of women with the sacred and the good. And the Assumption too can represent a categorical 'no' to the peculiar association of women with sin-flesh-matter[6] in the context of a religion which proclaims incarnation but which is sometimes anti-incarnational, anti-sacramental, and in which grace may be treated as a denial of the creature instead of its blessing. The Assumption helps to redress the balance in a dramatic way, giving some sense to Cornelius Ernst's remark that 'grace is not faceless'[7]—that is, the face can be female as well as male.

The trouble is, that women have all too consistently been allied with the old Eve, rather than with the new one, and this has been done by undercutting the ideal of whole personhood. This can be illustrated in the first instance by attending to an example given by Nelle Morton in her book, *The Journey is Home*.[8] In one of her essays, she describes a sculpture in wood outside a church building, a sculpture on the theme of vocation taken from 1 Cor. 10:31, 'Whether therefore ye eat, or drink, or whatsoever ye do, do all to the glory of God'. The sculpture shows thirty individual forms representing nineteen different kinds of work. Only seven of the thirty figures are women, represented as nursing a baby, on knees scrubbing a floor, serving a man seated at table, assisting a male doctor, feeding chickens, pounding a typewriter, and teaching children. All these figures represent tasks that arguably need doing, but it is absurd to associate that necessity with women alone, and absurd to exclude them from connection with the other twenty-three figures representing nineteen kinds of work. It needs little imagination to think out the likely roles of the male figures in the sculpture. The point is that as well as at one level honouring women and teaching them new aspirations, the Christian tradition has also undercut that honour and aspiration by teaching women a disabling gender construction, and this is why it has by no means always fostered whole personhood in women. Not surprisingly, it is now regarded as one of the sources of 'sexism', that is, the belief that persons are superior or inferior to one another on the basis of their sex.

It might be better to refer to the problem as gender-stereotyping. For we can distinguish between 'sex' and 'gender' in the following way. Sex has to do with basic biological differences which develop in a human embryo at about the sixth week of development. 'Gender' refers to what a particular society makes of relationships between males and females and no society lives free of gender constructs in all their astonishing variability. What one can do at the least is to attend to them and evaluate them, especially as these are conveyed by religious symbols, as realities which may help us to lay hold of or be laid hold of by realities beyond those which we see or think about. The object is not to obliterate differences, but to value them appropriately, and this need not mean that all those associated with males or masculinity are put at the top of some hierarchy of value, with those associated with females or femininity put at the bottom. It can be argued that notwithstanding some of the meanings associated with the symbol of Mary, the dominant gender construction of Christian culture for women has been that they are passive, dependent, bodily, emotional, weak, peculiarly responsible for evil and sin, are childlike in the worst senses, and bear the image of God only derivatively . Men, on the other hand, are active, independent, intelligent, brave, strong, good, bear the image of God in their own right, and are of course godlike. Males are always more godlike than females could ever be, even when the latter try religiously sanctioned experiments of trying to approximate to males.[9]

To claim that 'in the whole of human instinct and understanding it is the masculine which is associated with giving and the feminine with receiving' (to cite the words of one of the patrons of the Ecumenical Society of the Blessed Virgin Mary) is as intolerable and bad for men as it is dishonest about women. Human beings each need to give and receive from one another in as open and reciprocal way as they can. Women who internalize the dominant gender construction have to engage in a very painful process of giving it up. As with the tasks represented by the sculpture, and giving and receiving, so passivity, dependence, bodiliness, emotion, acknowledging weakness, etc. are arguably as important aspects of being human as being active, independent, intelligent, brave, strong and so on, and it is damaging to associate these possibilities primarily with one sex rather than another, regardless of time, place and circumstance. Yet it is probably harder to give up playing Cinderella, Snow White or Sleeping Beauty, than to give up playing Prince Charming, since this involves taking responsibility for oneself, rather than continuing with the symptoms of what is sometimes called co-dependence: low self-esteem, an inability to take care of oneself, wasting time thinking about what other people want, deluding oneself into thinking oneself responsible for its delivery, and that whatever goes wrong is one's personal responsibility to put right. Women, like men, need boundaries, permeable indeed, but secure, knowing what they think and feel from the inside, which is part of what feminist praxis is about. Once the boundaries are found, women can move through the limitations set for them by those who may not have their interests at heart.

One illustration of how this could work, drawing on the symbol of Mary, was given in an essay by Lavinia Byrne,[10] a good example of someone who wants to make constructive use of some of the paradoxes of the tradition. The paradoxes are well set out by Peter Canisius in the sixteenth century:

> A virgin not sterile, but fertile; married to a man, but made fruitful by God; bearing a son, but knowing not a man; forever inviolate, yet not deprived of progeny. A virgin pregnant but incorrupt, and intact even in childbirth. A virgin before marriage and in marriage, a pregnant virgin, a virgin giving suck, a perpetual virgin. A virgin without concupiscence conceiving the saviour. A virgin bearing a child in the womb without hardship, giving birth to God without pain.[11]

Lavinia Byrne must, as with others dealing with the legacy of the symbol, be both selective, and a translator, re-interpreter of the tradition, because Mary, as in the quotation from Canisius, is otherwise an impossible ideal for women. To be true to her tradition, she has to allow 'virginity' and 'motherhood' both to stand as reality, but also use them as metaphor for the experience of all women. Virginity as metaphor is about separation, and motherhood as metaphor is about integration.

> A woman who holds both of these in balance demonstrates the sanctifying power of differentiation. She is both apart from and

part of the human condition. The virgin is the reserved figure who does not define herself in terms of her relationships with men. She is autonomous. The mother, meanwhile, is essentially in relationship. The virgin is barren through choice or misfortune. Her energy is inner-directed. The mother is fecund. She is creative of life and ongoing nurture.

Then she argues that women are entitled to space both in the domestic context and in the public domain, but 'space' means something different in each place, as it were. First, where some women are free to make vows of chastity, we are reminded that all women should be free to refuse men access to them. Second, space in the public domain means that 'women are entitled to the freedom to engage with and be part of all the creative, nurturing processes with which we organize human reality'. Women should be allowed to differentiate, enabled to experience desires they do not ordinarily give themselves credit for, and to exercise choices society is reluctant to admit.

Quite a different example of constructive reinterpretation can be found in the work of two Latin American religious, Ivone Gebara and Maria Clara Bingemer, in their *Mary: Mother of God, Mother of the Poor*.[12] Although the book attempts a near-impossible task of exercising a method of interpretation alien to those who constructed Roman Catholic dogmas about Mary in relation to those dogmas, the main thrust of the book is intelligible enough, and makes clear why those concerned with women's lives will associate Mary with them in so far as they can, in order to mobilize for change. It is not simply, though it is essential in the Latin American context, that whereas to invading Spaniards Mary represented the triumph of conquest, to the despairing Indians lamenting the destruction of their religion and culture she represented the promise of a new life.[13] It is also that women across national boundaries are becoming alert to their predicament, in the words of the UN in 1980, that 'Women constitute half the world's population, perform nearly two-thirds of its work hours, receive one-tenth of the world's income, and own less than one-hundredth of the world's property'. Central to their predicament is that they are poor not because they bear children, but because they also have to do most of the work in raising them. Women experience in an acute form the conflict between the public-economic and the domestic which simply does not allow for support for the next generation, of the fragile and of the aging, and sentimentality about Mary should in no circumstances render their plight worse.

This is certainly not the intention of the authors of this book. For them, above all, Mary is one who 'lives in God', who expresses or embodies an unlimited yearning for life. She participates wholly and fully in the glory of the living God, rescued from humiliation, but has to do with saving life in the here and now. So the authors write that life is such a tough battle, that the relationship with Mary, she who is 'alive in God', full of affection and power, is direct. It is connected to people's immediate and vital needs, 'since the life of the poor unfolds basically at this level'.[14] So too Anne Carr, in *Transforming Grace* writes of Mary as the poor one in whom God does great things:

> Mary as virgin and mother need not be understood as an impossible double bind, an inimitable ideal, but as a central Christian symbol that signifies autonomy and relationship, strength and tenderness, struggle and victory, God's power and human agency—not in competition but co-operation; Mary is a utopian figure, a mystery. Her intimate place in the Christian pattern enables us to imagine a healed, reconciled, finally transformed world.[15]

These writers are all alert to some of the dangers associated with the symbol of Mary, including idealized femininity from a male viewpoint, and Mary as 'mother' of the Church strengthening the religious and cultural foundations of androcentrism which has not attended to women, heard their voices, or been humanly inclusive in a consistent way in its institutions or its theology. James Mackey has shrewdly pointed out[16] (referring to the book by Ivone Gebara and Maria Clara Bingemer) that images, metaphors and symbols are based on some actual state of affairs from which the range of significance is extended to bring to light a greater range of actual or possible experience. The authors quoted in this essay are engaged in that process of extension. But, as Mackey goes on:

> Virginity, as an image or symbol, has its basis in a genital sexual state, and it symbolizes closedness, if anything at all, certainly not openness; and the failure so far to realize any possibilities whatsoever. It forces imagery beyond the range of intelligibility to suggest otherwise; and it borders on the perverse to choose the virgin rather than the married woman as a symbol of fidelity.

Be that as it may (and Peter Brown for one shows us how in the fourth century, for instance, virginal integrity represented sacralized culture, and literacy),[17] Mackey makes effectively some of the points women have been making about the use and abuse of the symbol to keep women in their place, particularly within the Church, though he, like others, remains hopeful that our symbols of divine, effective and saving power can have a transforming impact on us. We need a renewed vision of goodness, to be given and to gain access to it, in both Church and society, a new sense of co-inherence between women and men, so that each actualizes the dignity and worth of the other, and the symbol of Mary may help us to achieve this. Preoccupation with the symbol may also help us not to attend to one central issue for the tradition, however, that is, its failure to take seriously a point made from time to time. We may pick up the point in some words of Elaine Storkey's, where she writes that:

> there is nothing demeaning in the notion of Mary bearing her own Saviour. It is not an assertion of the supremacy of maleness or the arrogance of patriarchy. It is simply a statement of the humility of a non-gendered God who was prepared to come in human, sexual form.[18]

The crucial phrase is 'the humility of a non-gendered God', for the main goal of feminist theology is a humanly inclusive theology, and the hope and necessity that we can envision the mystery of God in gender-inclusive ways. As Elizabeth Johnson properly insists,[19] this is not a matter of adding a female-related or feminine dimension to a God imaged as male or masculine, but the claim that the female and feminine can of and by itself image God, in as full and in as limited a way as God is imaged by the male and masculine. Both sexes and genders are as capable or incapable of imaging the mystery of God. In Elizabeth Johnson's reflections on Mary as symbol, therefore, she retrieves the creativity and caring intrinsic to good mothering; compassion as primordially divine; saving and protective power; the immanence and living presence of God—Gerard Manley Hopkins' 'Wild air, world mothering air'. We might add what Hannah Arendt in her political philosophy called natality, the capacity for new beginnings, so closely related to the capacity for forgiveness.[20] For Elizabeth Johnson, ways of referring to the mystery of God which could be received within a believing community include maternity with its nurturing and warmth; unbounded compassion; power that protects, heals and liberates all-embracing immanence; and recreative energy.

Mary then is one way of referring to the mystery of God, but that she does, or in so far as she does, should not be allowed to shift our focus from this central task, and unless it is achieved, it is at least arguable that the future vitality of the tradition is at stake. Concentrating on the symbol of Mary to the exclusion of this task will not save it, or at least, it may not be as good as it could be, for men as well as women.

NOTES TO CHAPTER 2

[1] See also Ann Loades, 'The Virgin Mary in the Feminist Quest', in Janet Martin Soskice, ed., *After Eve* (London: Collins, 1990), pp. 156-78 (a paper for the Ecumenical Society of the Blessed Virgin Mary and other similar groups).

[2] David F. Wright, ed., *Chosen by God: Mary in Evangelical Perspective* (London: Marshall Pickering, 1989) provides some recent examples.

[3] *Redemptoris Mater*, para. 46.

[4] Nicholas Perry and Loreto Echeverria, *Under the Heel of Mary* (London: Routledge, 1988).

[5] Donal Flanagan, 'Mary: Some Problems in Ambivalence', in Alberic Stacpoole, ed., *Mary and the Churches* (Dublin: Columba, 1987), pp. 73-84.

[6] See the references in Loades, 'The Virgin Mary and the Feminist Quest'.

[7] Cornelius Ernst, *Multiple Echo* (London: Darton, Longman and Todd, 1979), p. 124.

[8] Nellie Morton, *The Journey is Home* (Boston, Mass.: Beacon, 1983), pp. 21-22.

[9] See, for instance, Avril Cameron, 'Virginity as Metaphor: Women and the Rhetoric of Early Christianity', in Avril Cameron, ed., *History as Text: The Writing of Ancient History* (London: Duckworth, 1989), pp. 181-205; Elizabeth Castelli, 'Virginity and its Meaning for Women's Sexuality in Early Christianity', *Journal of Feminist Studies in Religion* 2 (1986): 61-88.

[10] Lavinia Byrne, 'Apart From or A Part Of: The Place of Celibacy', in Alison Joseph, ed., *Through the Devil's Gateway: Women, Religion and Taboo* (London: SPCK, 1990).

[11] Ian MacLean, *The Renaissance Notion of Women* (Cambridge: Cambridge University Press, 1980), p. 29.

[12] Ivone Gebara and Maria Clara Bingemer, *Mary: Mother of God, Mother of the Poor* (Maryknoll, N.Y.: Orbis Books, 1989).

[13] Patricia Harrington, 'Mother of Death, Mother of Rebirth: The Mexican Virgin of Guadalupe', *Journal of the American Academy of Religion* 56 (1988): 25-50.

[14] Gebara and Bingemer, *Mary*, pp. 23, 119, 126.

[15] Anne Carr, *Transforming Grace* (San Francisco: Harper and Row, 1988), p. 193.

[16] James Mackey, 'The Use and Abuse of Mary in Roman Catholicism', in Richard Holloway, ed., *Who Needs Feminism? Men Respond to Sexism in the Church* (London: SPCK, 1991), pp. 99-116.

[17] Peter Brown, *The Body and Society* (London: Faber, 1989), especially pp. 259-284.

[18] Elaine Storkey, 'The Significance of Mary for Feminist Theology', in David Wright, ed., *Chosen by God: Mary in Evangelical Perspective* (London: Marshall Pickering, 1989), pp. 184-99, especially p. 198.

[19] Elizabeth Johnson, 'Mary and the Image of God', and 'Reconstructing a Theology of Mary', in Doris Donnelly, ed., *Mary: Woman of Nazareth* (Mahwah, N.J.: Paulist Press, 1989), pp. 25-68 and 69-91. See also Elizabeth Johnson, 'The Incomprehensibility of God and the Image of God Male and Female', in Joann Wolski Conn, ed., *Women's Spirituality: Resources for Christian Development* (Mahwah, N.J.: Paulist Press, 1986), pp. 243-260.

[20] Hannah Arendt, *The Human Condition* (New York, N.Y.: Doubleday, 1958), pp. 10-11 and 221-22.

3

Regarding Mary and the Trinity:
The Anglican Position

I: Introduction

I take the term 'Anglican' here to refer primarily to the Church of England, though I think that the positions to which I refer in this paper would also be found in the spectrum of most of its related episcopal churches, especially the Church in Wales and the Church of Ireland whose territory includes Northern Ireland, the Anglican Diocese of Europe, and the Episcopal Church of Scotland. I have no way of ascertaining the position of all the Churches of the world-wide Anglican Communion, though again I expect that within it I would find a similar range of theological conviction about Mary and the Trinity. We also need to bear in mind the existence of the Porvoo agreement with north European Lutheran Churches. The Evangelical-Lutheran Church of Latvia has not yet taken a decision on the Porvoo Declaration, and the Church of Denmark has decided not to endorse it but to maintain links with those who have. There are many difficult issues for discussion in such churches, but my point here is simply that discussion of 'the Trinity and Mary' is a sensitive issue not least in the Church of England's ecumenical negotiations, especially with those Churches with whom it is now in full communion.

The second point I need to make by way of introduction is that I do not write as an official spokesperson of the Church of England to the Twentieth Mariological Marian International Congress, though I hope I do justice to the complexities of my church's position as a member of its Doctrine Commission—not that at the moment the Commission is likely to discuss the relation between the Trinity and Mary. Relevant discussion, however, took place in the Church of England's Synod in 1998-2000, and I shall return to this later via the records of the discussion in Synod's Report of Proceedings. For those unfamiliar with Synod, it may be helpful to note that it has three 'Houses'—the House of Bishops, the House of Clergy, and the House of Laity. For any motion to be carried it is required that there be a two-thirds majority in each of the three Houses. The House of Bishops rightly does its best to present a united front to the Clergy and Laity when central points of doctrine are at issue, as in the 1998-2000 debates about the translation of the Nicene Creed to be used in the new liturgies. It was in the course of this debate that discussion of 'the Trinity and Mary' surfaced, as I have already indicated. It is also worth noting that just as the reports of the Doctrine Commission have to be presented to and approved by Synod, so does the work of the Liturgical Commission. In this case, however, it was the House of Bishops, and neither the Doctrine Commission nor the Liturgical Commission, which had to negotiate consensus about the truth with the rest of Synod, and it was with the House of Laity that they had most difficulty.

The importance of the voice of the laity in the church should not be underestimated. I know virtually nothing about the theological competence of the members of the House of Laity, but I do know a little about those whom they represent. These include people who are studying Christian theology at an academic level in Britain, the majority of whom (and of whatever Church) are now lay, some of them teaching theology professionally. There are also many lay people serving the Church as Readers, taking non-eucharistic services, leading intercessions and preaching, or having some other authorised liturgical role. There are more of them than there are full-time ordained clergy. And, importantly, there are the laity of the parishes, some of them sustained by the *Book of Common Prayer*. Clergy and laity together have all had about twenty years' familiarisation with the *Alternative Service Book 1980*, though ameliorated somewhat by the reintroduction of the *Book of Common Prayer* Collects in modern English. At the turn of the millennium they were faced with yet another round of liturgical revision. Tensions about these revisions may well have found a focus on the translation of the Nicene Creed, and hence on the relationship of Mary to the Trinity. Since, so far as I know, most of us learn our doctrine through our liturgical life and its associated 'devotions', it is of course important that the formal and the informal do not pull too far apart, and, in addition, that we work with genuine and deep respect for our differences. Reading the record of the Synod debates, I think that such respect was exemplified despite the tensions.

II: Some historical reflections

It would not be to the point here for me to narrate in detail the fate of two inter-related sets of convictions and their associated practices—those concerning Mary, and those concerning the invocation of the saints—which can be traced in the history of the Prayer Books between 1544 and 1662, but it is necessary to recall certain points of importance. These are that the Prayer Books reflect the protests of Reformers against whatever seemed to obscure the priority and centrality of Christ's redemptive work, the authority of Scripture relative to other authorities, and the doctrines of salvation and justification. What eventually remained in the *Book of Common Prayer* and associated liturgical books was far from negligible, even if unsatisfying. We attend to begin with to the Feast of the Nativity and its Trinitarian Collect:

> Almighty God, who hast given us thy only-begotten Son to take our nature upon him, and as at this time to be born of a pure Virgin; grant that we being regenerate, and made thy children by adoption and grace, may daily be renewed by thy Holy Spirit; through the same our Lord Jesus Christ, who liveth and reigneth with thee and the same Spirit, ever one God, world without end.

The liturgy for Christmas Day refers in its Proper Preface to Christ's being made 'very man of the substance of the Virgin Mary his mother, and that without spot of sin, to make us clean from all sin'. The Feasts of Annunciation and Purification were retained as 'Red Letter' days with 'Propers' (so-called because of the colour of ink used to highlight them, and now taken to require a eucharistic celebration); the Visitation, Mary's own Conception and her Nativity were retained as 'Black Letter' days. The Feast of Mary's Nativity on 8 September has for many Anglicans remained the principal Marian Feast, perhaps because as her own 'official birthday' it could focus primarily on Mary herself rather than on Christ in the first instance. Of course, the Gospel for the Annunciation is the expected passage from St Luke, but neither its Collect, nor that of the other Feasts, associates Mary in particular with the Trinity. Nor, despite Acts 1:14, does that for the Feast of Pentecost. In my view this is a significant and serious omission from the Prayer Books and liturgies of any church, not just for understanding Mary herself, but for the place and authority of women in the Church at large—a point to which I shall return. The Collect for All Saints' Day addresses God as the one 'who has knit together thine elect in one communion and fellowship, in the mystical body of thy Son Christ our Lord', and goes on to petition God as follows:

> Grant us grace so to follow thy blessed Saints in all virtuous and godly living that we may come to those unspeakable joys, which thou hast prepared for them that unfeignedly love thee; through Jesus Christ our Lord.

The Epistle is from Revelation, but not, of course, 'the woman clothed with the sun'.[1] Self-evidently, Mary is not specially identified, and number XXII of the Articles of Religion, 'Of Purgatory' declares that 'invocation of Saints' is repugnant to the Word of God, and 'purgatory' remains a contested concept. Article XXII apart, the implication of the collect for All Saints' Day is also that the saints are not to be 'invoked', if that means asking for their aid as if they have power to act on our behalf independently of Christ. Underpinning particular points in the liturgical year with their associated prayers and readings, at Matins and Evensong generations of Anglicans have said or sung the Apostles' Creed: 'conceived by (Latin *de*) the Holy Ghost, born of (*ex*) the Virgin Mary',—two different prepositions as in the Latin of the Nicene Creed of the eucharist. At Evensong said or sung on a daily basis in one of innumerable settings is the *Magnificat*, prayed as it were with Mary herself. In the twentieth and twenty-first centuries, it must be noted that so far as parish (as distinct from Cathedral) worship is concerned, to the extent that the eucharist has displaced both Matins and Evensong, the focus has increasingly been on the Nicene Creed: 'And was incarnate by the Holy Ghost of the Virgin Mary, and was made man'.

If we look at the period before and after 1662 and the restoration of the monarchy and the *Book of Common Prayer*, there is unambiguous evidence of the discomfort and disquiet of at least some of the clergy, and we may suppose some of their parishioners, about what was on offer to them so far as Mary was concerned. I give here only three examples.[2] My three are as follows. John Donne, Dean of St Paul's Cathedral in London, who died in 1631, wrote in his poem 'A Litanie' of Mary that 'As her deeds were / Our helpes, so are her prayers: nor can she sue / In vaine, who hath such titles unto you'. From the fact that Donne believed Mary's prayers to be effective it did not of course follow that he could or would do more than pray that his prayers might be associated with hers. It is in that sense that he might 'invoke' her, not that he could appeal to her because he dared not appeal to

Christ directly. One of Donne's special friends—twenty years younger than he—was another great priest-poet, George Herbert, who died only two years later than Donne, in 1633. In the central section of 'To All Angels and Saints' Herbert explicitly says to Mary: 'Chiefly to thee would I my soul unfold', yet continues: 'But now (alas!) I dare not; for our King, / Whom we do all jointly adore and praise / Bids no such thing'. My third example is taken from the work of a man whose work was one of the most astonishing discoveries of the late nineteenth century onwards, a third priest-poet, Thomas Traherne, born after the death of Donne and Herbert (and dying in 1674). Traherne was reared and educated under the Protestant Commonwealth, first commissioned as a minister according to Parliamentary regulation, then episcopally ordained into the Established Church at the Restoration, and thenceforward nourished by the *Book of Common Prayer*. He is arguably the most ecstatic priest-poet of them all. It is part of one of his devotions which is now included as one of those to be used by the Ecumenical Society of the Blessed Virgin Mary.[3] Traherne's devotion begins:

And first O Lord I praise and magnify thy Name
For the Most Holy Virgin-Mother of GOD, who is the Highest of thy Saints.
The most Glorious of all thy Creatures.
The most Perfect of all thy Works.
The nearest unto Thee, in the Throne of God.
Whom Thou didst please to make
Daughter of the Eternal Father.
Mother of the Eternal Son.
Spouse of the Eternal Spirit.
Tabernacle of the most Glorious Trinity.

It continues with seven lines of praise of her as 'Mother' with biblical titles, and another five lines of praise of her as 'Mirror' of nine biblical virtues: 'Mirror of all virtues' is the apt conclusion of this first part. Traherne goes on to sum up and as it were to comment on his praise of Mary, for he writes: 'The most illustrious Light in the Church, Wearing over all her Beauties the veil of Humility to shine the more resplendently in thy Eternal Glory. And yet this Holy virgin-Mother styled herself but the Handmaid of the Lord, and falls down with all the Glorious Hosts of Angels, and with the Armies of Saints, at the foot of Thy throne, to worship and Glorify Thee for ever and ever'. He indeed praises God 'for doing in Her all thy Merciful Works for my sake, and the Benefit of Mankind', but does not isolate her from all those who hear the Word of God and keep it, becoming Christ's brother/

sister/mother by doing the Will of God. The 'Glorious Graces' given and imparted to 'this Holy Virgin' were given to 'all thy Saints', and in response to these and God's own excellencies and perfection Traherne summons himself to worship. Quite apart from Traherne's own knowledge of Roman Catholic devotional language in this period, the continued availability of Dante's *Divine Comedy*, suffused as it is with 'Marian' texts and convictions, may well have sustained familiarity with the kind of language Traherne used in the first part of his devotion. Quite apart from anything else, my examples from the seventeenth-century provide me with an opportunity to make what seems to me to be a very important point, which is about how much liturgy and the very possibility of learning doctrine depends not just on such poets, but on musicians, sculptors, painters and workers in many crafts who are as such themselves discriminating and perceptive theologians. I also think that the capacities they exemplify to one degree or another are also required of the 'performers' of liturgies, though there is no time to explore this point here. To give only one example, the capacity of musicians to explore the significance of the *Magnificat* across the centuries seems to me essential to keep the freshness of the words alive for all who participate in the liturgies where it is used in a way that reciting the words alone could not do.

In rehearsing some examples from the post-Reformation Church of England, however, one should also note the difficulties which continued to bear on some people in different centuries and circumstances. To many in nineteenth century Britain, for instance, Mary continued to symbolise superstition and idolatry.[4] Those who found her to be central to their life as believers had to make their convictions known with some caution. It is arguable that John Keble exemplifies the problem. The heir of those seventeenth-century priest-poets already mentioned (and of many others to whom reference could be made) as well as of the *Book of Common Prayer*, he wrote a poem in 1844 significantly called 'Mother out of sight'. On the advice of his friends he omitted it from a collection of his poetry published in 1846, but eventually published it in a collection of his miscellaneous poems. Keble had moved himself beyond George Herbert's reluctance and thinks that we may at least like children say 'Aye' to Christ's mother. For as he wrote:

> Angel nor Saint His face may see
> Apart from What He took of thee.
> How may we choose but name thy name
> Echoing below their high acclaim
> In holy Creeds?

And yet we also find in this poem the sense of discretion which I suggest still characterises Anglican devotion to Mary. The first line of Keble's poem indeed addresses her as 'Mother of God', and with her he wishes to magnify the Lord and bring her near 'with all the saints'. He incorporates 'Hail Mary, full of grace!' into his fifth stanza, and in his sixth refers to her as 'enthroned Spouse, / His Church and Bride'. His discretion appears in his second stanza:

> What glory thou above hast now,
> By special grace of thy dear Son,
> We see not yet, nor dare espy
> Thy crowned form with open eye.
> Rather beside the manger meek
> Thee bending with veiled brow we seek,
> Or where the Angel in the thrice-great-Name
> Hail'd thee and Jesus to thy bosom came.

We may suppose that Keble seems to be aware that conspicuous by its absence from the *Book of Common Prayer*, and indeed from the 1980 *Alternative Service Book*, was the Feast of the Assumption to which Keble clearly alludes, as did Traherne. If we ask how they came to know of it, the answer may well be that both learned of it at the University of Oxford, since it survived in that University's Calendar despite the Reformation. Whether or how it was celebrated in Christ Church, at once Cathedral and College Chapel, or anywhere else in Oxford in the middle of the long vacation, I simply do not know. Keble cannot, however, make it central to his devotion – 'Mother' may be greeted, and sought, but not directly adored as one seen in full glory. And Keble's sense of discretion is still arguably present in the Church of England, for although the Feast of the Assumption is now back as a 'Red Letter' day in the Church of England's Calendar (thus catching up with Scottish Episcopalians in their 1928 Prayer Book), the Feast on August 15 is simply indicated as for 'The Blessed Virgin Mary' as in the American Episcopal Prayer Book of 1979 (which, however, does not commemorate her own nativity on 8 September). As with other saints, the day of Mary's death is now commemorated, and this means that at last the Church of England has restored the Feast which is most significant for the dedication of some of our Cathedrals as well as parish churches, did they but know it, since unless some other feast is specified in a dedication to Mary, it is this one which is being honoured. Long before the official restoration of the Feast, some twentieth century Anglicans at least (depending on which hymn book they use) have in fact been singing it, for the second stanza of

Athelstan Riley's 'Ye watchers and ye holy ones' (well known in a splendid setting by Ralph Vaughan Williams) goes as follows:

> O higher than the Cherubim,
> More glorious than the Seraphim,
> Lead their praises, Alleluia!
> Thou Bearer of the eternal Word,
> Most gracious, magnify the Lord,
> Alleluia!

Anglicans are certainly short of prayers for the Feast, having 'mislaid' them a long time ago, as well as lacking a wealth of earlier imagery associated with Mary, but not everything was lost, as that hymn for one indicates. The restoration of the Feast of the Assumption minus some if not all of its decor, as it were, is a logical follow-on from the agreement reached by the Anglican and Roman Catholic International Commission (ARCIC) on the content of Marian dogmas: 'Mary, the Mother of God incarnate (*Theotokos*), was prepared by divine grace to be the mother of our Redeemer, by whom she was herself redeemed, and received into glory.'

III: Some doctrinal reflections

It is clear from the ARCIC agreement that to celebrate the Feast of the Assumption does not require assent to the controversial dogma of the Immaculate Conception. To focus on that dogma, however briefly, I suggest that a helpful essay referring to it is by Rowan Williams. Williams writes of its point without endorsing it as a dogma:

> What Jesus, humanly speaking, grew up into was made possible by his closest human contacts; so that what he is able to give God through his human will and understanding is what is given to his developing humanity by those who first nurture him. If Jesus is able to live in a way that means that all his dealings are, without obstacle, open to God, this must (in the ordinary processes of human development) be enabled by what is given to him by the first human other he encounters. And that first human other is Mary. At the foundation of Jesus' historical humanity lie his relationships with his parents but, more particularly, with Mary; hers is the first human face he will in any real sense be aware of. What he sees there is crucial to how he sees God.[5]

His point is that if Christ's humanity was exceptional, the conditions of his learning it must have been in some way exceptional, with Mary at the centre of it. She herself so lives in relation to God and others that she makes her son uniquely free for God and others also. Her role is not only her free consent at the Annunciation, but the way in which her freedom makes room for God throughout her life. She makes possible for him in his particularity something already real at the centre of his being, which is 'the given, abiding presence of God the Word, the real relation of divine love to divine love that is eternal in heaven.' Mary enables in him a humanity in which there is no obstacle to that divine self-expression.[6]

True to the dogma, Williams' exposition is also valuable in the way it makes a number of useful points. He emphasises the inter-dependence and intra-dependence of human beings with one another, but also Mary's freedom. We may all appreciate the determination of theologians as diverse as Karl Barth and Hans Urs von Balthasar to dislodge all traces of human pride and self-assertion from our understanding of Mary's assent to God's 'proposal' at the Annunciation, but we have no need, so far as I know, to turn Mary of all human beings, into some kind of door-mat if we are even to begin to understand her son. Although Williams does not say so, we may add to his explicit concerns one for recognition of the full human dignity of women, given that Mary's bodiliness remains held to the centre of divine and sacred life, for what is true for her may be true for other women specifically, and not merely for undifferentiated 'humanity'. Touched on in Williams' work is Mary's own discipleship, existing necessarily from before the Annunciation, which makes her assent intelligible, but carried on throughout her life in relation to, and mutual interaction with, her son up to Pentecost and beyond, including the 'beyond' of her Assumption. This theme of her discipleship received sustained and substantial treatment in the two books published by David Brown arising from his 1996 Hensley Henson Lectures in Oxford. His two books are of major importance for anyone concerned with Anglican doctrinal theology. In *Tradition and Imagination: Revelation and Change* (1999) there is a chapter on 'Pentecost and Crib'; and in *Discipleship and Imagination: Christian Tradition and Truth* (2000) there is a chapter on 'Mary and Virgin Promise'.[7] Even here, however, there is so to speak, an unfinished line of development. Given that the earliest known image of Pentecost is that from the Rabbula Gospels (from the monastery of St John of Zagba in Syria) of 586AD and that this image places Mary at the heart and centre of the disciples (as in Acts 1:14) as did many another for some centuries, we may well ask about the evangelistic mission for women that this image of Pentecost suggests. Mary's discipleship may have included not merely recognition of Christ's resurrection and Spirit-giving but its active proclamation, perhaps made doubly hard for her because she would have to meet the grief of the mothers whose own sons had been done to death by the Herods and Pilates of this world. Her predecessor in the hope of resurrection was the mother of the Maccabean martyrs (2 Maccabees 7), but Mary would be the one to bear the burden of proclaiming its reality. One very powerful visual image of what is being suggested here is Elizabeth Fink's immensely powerful statue of Mary outside Salisbury Cathedral, walking away from it, still marked in face and body by grief, but off and out of her familiar world to proclaim the resurrection—apostolic witness in the New Testament sense. I have yet to come across one single post-Vatican II discussion of Marian doctrine which makes this proposal, no doubt because its consequences for the responsibilities of women for the preaching and teaching of the gospel would be intolerable to some, and perhaps burdensome to women themselves. There can be deep resistance to the summons such a 'Mary' represents by women as well as men, within Anglicanism as well as in other churches.[8]

IV: Concluding observations

That remark brings me to this final part, which is concerned with what I learned from my reading of the 1998-2000 debates in the Church of England's Synod. Recall that I said earlier that Anglicans have been used in the *Book of Common Prayer* to 'conceived by (*de*) the Holy Ghost, born of (*ex*) the Virgin Mary' in the Apostles' Creed; and at the eucharist to 'And was incarnate by the Holy Ghost of the Virgin Mary' in the Nicene Creed. In addition, in the *Alternative Service Book*, they learned a version of the Nicene Creed which introduced a paraphrase, and interpretation of 'by the Holy Ghost' which read 'by the power of the Holy Spirit'. Two different prepositions, then, to mark the difference between the Holy Spirit and Mary, and the first prepositional phrase interpreted (I understand) as suggested by the International Consultation on English Texts. The interpreted clause incorporates as 'translation' what is proper to 'instruction', though the Nicene Creed it should be noted was never intended as a creed for uninstructed beginners, but for those who are least likely to confuse the respective roles of the Spirit and Mary.

Round one of Synod debate in November 1998 went to those who wanted to retain 'by the power of the Holy Spirit' for which of course there was no precedent before the 1960s/1970s, for what precedents are worth. Round two in February 2000 almost went to the Bishops and clergy who wanted to be faithful to the *original* language of the Nicene Creed and not to its Latin and later English translations with two distinct prepositions. The Greek text of the Nicene Creed ran: *kai sarkothenta ek Pneumatos Hagiou kai Marias tes Parthenou*; and as translated by the English Language Liturgical Commission (ELLC) correctly with the one preposition governing both genitives: 'and was incarnate of the Holy Spirit and the Virgin Mary'. The problem was that bishops and clergy could not get the laity to agree with them at the two-thirds majority level, no matter what was said about the point and purpose of this part of the Nicene Creed. They saw no reason to concede the ELLC translation, given their familiarity with the Latin/English version in use for centuries. If the issue was one of returning to the original language of the Nicene Creed, then another question of a radical kind about 'origins' could be asked, which was whether the Greek of the Nicene Creed quite did justice to the texts of St Matthew and Galatians. If the argument was to move in the direction of development rather than in appeal to origins, there could be justification for the introduction in the Latin west of two different prepositions to distinguish between the roles of the Spirit and Mary, and there could then be justification for a further move in that direction, such as 'by the power of the Holy Spirit'. And, persistently throughout the debate, some supposed that what was at stake was precisely the exaltation of the role of Mary.

Bishops and clergy finally persuaded enough of the laity in February 2000 to accept the one preposition Nicene Creed. The price was to drop the ELLC 'of the Holy Spirit and the Virgin Mary' and agree on 'was incarnate from the Holy Spirit and the Virgin Mary'. One justification for the translation of *ek* as 'from' was that it was familiar from Anglican Patristic scholarship. Far more important seems to have been the claim that 'from' was deemed to indicate the 'beyondness', transcendence and creativity of the Holy Spirit, but could not indicate anything of the kind in respect of Mary. I think that an Anglican 'Trinity and Mary' theology can and must do better than this. I have already said that it should certainly embrace the implications of Pentecost if we are to be 'biblical'. My conclusion, however, turns us back to Mary at the point in her discipleship indicated by the word 'Annunciation'. We need to probe further questions of the interrelationship of Spirit, grace and nature that to a large extent are put on one side if we are talking here of 'beyondness' and transcendence. I concentrate instead here on 'creativity', since I remain entirely at a loss in reading theologians who deny Mary (and by implication, other women) even a shred of creativity in her consent to pregnancy, a pregnancy which might result not only in her abandonment and ostracism, but, given the conditions of her time, even in her own death. Persuasive definition, no doubt, but if consent to pregnancy is not about creativity, generosity and self-gift, even before we begin to think of the nurture and up-bringing of a child safely born, it is difficult to imagine what is. We must, I think, suppose that Mary was a girl of remarkable courage, and we might begin a renewed Marian theology with her courage and creativity in mind. It is in these graces that the divine Spirit meets with and meshes with hers, not to overwhelm her, any more than she overwhelmed her son, but to enhance the freedom which was already hers, a freedom which cannot be enjoyed on a pedestal, but eventually takes her to apostolic life as an evangelist.

NOTES TO CHAPTER 3

[1] For a relevant essay see Ian Boxall. 'Who is the Woman Clothed with the Sun?' in Martin Warner, ed., *Say Yes to God. Mary and the Revealing of the Word Made Flesh* (London: Tufton, 1999), pp. 142-158.

[2] For others, see A. M. Allchin, *The Joy of All Creation. An Anglican Meditation on the Place of Mary* (London: Darton, Longman and Todd, 1984).

[3] My quotations are taken from John E. Barnes, 'A Caroline Devotion to the Virgin Mary', *Theology* 73 (1970): 535-541.

[4] See John Singleton, 'The Virgin Mary and Religious Conflict in Victorian Britain', *Journal of Ecclesiastical History* 43 (1992): 16-34.

[5] Rowan Williams, '"The Seal of Orthodoxy": Mary and the Heart of Christian Doctrine', in Martin Warner, ed., *Say Yes to God: Mary and the Revealing of the Word Made Flesh* (London: Tufton, 1999), pp. 15-29, at pp. 19-20.

[6] Williams, 'Seal of Orthodoxy', p. 21.

[7] David W. Brown, *Tradition and Imagination: Revelation and Change* (Oxford: Oxford University Press, 1999); David W. Brown, *Discipleship and Imagination: Christian Tradition and Truth* (Oxford: Oxford University Press, 2000).

[8] Apart from David Brown's essays in his two books listed above, see also Elizabeth A. Johnson's particularly fine essay, 'The Symbolic Character of Theological Statements about Mary', *Journal of Ecumenical Studies* 22 (1985): 312-335 for a possible theological framework in which to reconfigure Mary for our time.

4

Bone of Contention

The 2005 Anglican-Roman Catholic International Commission (ARCIC) 'agreed statement' on 'Mary' is self-acknowledged as 'an ecclesial and ecumenical reading' (para. 7)[1] and is at one level commendable in its endeavour to draw upon what is referred to as 'the whole tradition of the Church' (para. 7).[2] Reference is then made to the unity and consistency of divine revelation and thus the way in which events and images may be understood, with specific reference to Christ; to emphases on the clarity and sufficiency of Scripture and the centrality of the Gospel message; to those approaches which attempt to discern the meaning intended by the biblical authors and to account for texts' origins; and to the range of possible readings of a text. The members of the Commission recognize that no reading is neutral, but that each is shaped by the context and interest of its readers, and with that recognition they 'seek to integrate what is valuable' from the various approaches in the interest of 'communion' (para. 8).[3] It will become clear in the course of this chapter that there is at least one major approach which is completely ignored by the Commission, presumably because it is not yet deemed to be part of the 'tradition'. 'Unity and consistency of revelation' can be selectively exclusive as well as inclusive. That apart, not every point made in the ARCIC document can be attended to here—my comments are necessarily selective.[4]

The interest of the ARCIC group in 'communion' informs the text in the sense that paragraphs 52-57[5] are distinctly 'Pauline' in their reliance on the scriptural pattern of predestination, calling, justification and glorification in such texts as Rom. 8:30: A Pauline perspective on 'Mary' is unusual but helpful it would appear, so that the Commission worked with an eschatological perspective, focused on Christ's own Ascension and the destiny of the Church and of its members (para. 53).[6] This enables a fresh reading of the 'economy of grace' from its fulfillment retrospectively, and enables the members of ARCIC to negotiate one of the 'bones of contention' between some Protestants on the one hand, and both Roman Catholics and the Orthodox communion on the other, with regard to Mary's Dormition or Assumption—by no means quite identical in meaning.[7] It is worth noting that in an earlier paragraph (para. 6) 'the whole sweep of salvation history' includes 'creation, election, the Incarnation, passion and resurrection of Christ, the gift of the Spirit in the Church, and the final vision of eternal life for all God's people in the new creation.'[8] In other words, at that point the text reveals the familiar neglect of the significance of Christ's Ascension in doctrinal theology, with unacknowledged implications for the understanding and reconfiguration of both 'sacrament' and the 'sacramental'. The document nowhere attends to the profound ambiguities of '*communio sanctorum*' in the Latin of the Apostles' Creed. Whilst the authors have much to say about the 'communion of saints', i.e. communion of sanctified persons, they do not explore the other sense of the phrase— communion in sanctified or consecrated things.

For the moment, however, it is important to attend to the place[9] where the authors say of the dogma of Mary's Assumption that she was 'assumed body and soul' and this can be seen to have 'Christological and ecclesiological implications. Mary as "God bearer" is intimately, indeed bodily, related to Christ: his own bodily glorification now embraces hers. And since Mary bore his body of flesh, she is intimately related to the Church, Christ's body'.[10] A bolder 'Marian' perspective could well yield a different emphasis here, in teasing out Christological implications. For since Christ became and remains through God's recreative grace incarnate 'from the Holy Spirit and the Virgin Mary'[11] his Ascension is a crucial symbol of divine redemptive presence continually available to us in transformative Spirit and sacrament. It is necessary not to lose sight of the meaning of Mary as '*Theotokos*' ('God-bearer') in respect of the Ascension. His humanity is that through which our own salvation is mediated, and that humanity is 'hers' uniquely. Thus, we might say that theologically she remains central and not peripheral to human hope for continued blessing and transformation of human life. It is insufficient to lose sight of her importance for ecclesiology, though as this chapter will suggest in due course, not in the way indicated in the document presently under discussion with the 'genderization' of the Church as 'she', which seems to result from Jesus' dying words in St John's Gospel giving Mary 'a motherly role in the Church' with encouragement of the community of disciples to embrace her 'as a spiritual mother', these disciples then being called 'to care for the Church as mother' (paras. 26, 27).[12] The document continues with Mary post-Vatican II as 'a figure of the Church, her arms uplifted in prayer and praise, her hands open in receptivity and availability to the outpouring of the Holy Spirit'.[13] Towards the end of the document we find an entirely proper reminder that nothing must obscure the mediation of Christ alone between God and humankind, in the course of recovering and re-emphasizing the point of asking others to pray for us, as 'a means by which, in and through the Spirit, its power may be displayed' (para.68).[14] The same paragraph maintains that 'all ministries of the Church, especially those of Word and sacrament, mediate the grace of God through human beings'. We need to comment: true, up to a point, but 'human beings' is not a humanly inclusive phrase, and cannot be in a document agreed by any group which includes those who cannot see the argument from Incarnation for a fully humanly inclusive ministry, a matter to which we shall return. Who then are 'we' who are 'at one with Mary'? Men performing 'maternal' roles?

If we are at one with Mary, however, we are encouraged not only to praise God for what he has done in and through her, but praise God with her in singing the *Magnificat* and 'in the Eucharist, they pray with her as they do with all God's people, integrating their prayers in the great communion of saints', recognizing her place in the prayer of all the saints 'uttered before the throne of God in the heavenly liturgy (Rev. 8:3-4)'.[15] We may juxtapose this with the words of the papal 'Exhortation on the Eucharist'.[16] Paragraph 96 begins, 'May Mary Most Holy, the Immaculate Virgin, ark of the new and eternal covenant, accompany us on our way to meet the Lord who comes. In her we find realized most perfectly the essence of the Church'. The claim is then made that the Church sees in Mary ('Woman of the Eucharist') her finest icon, 'and she contemplates Mary as a singular model of the Eucharistic life'. The Pope reminds his readers that the priest honours Mary as he 'prepares to receive on the altar the *verum Corpus natum de Maria Virgine*', Mother of the Church, for she 'is the *tota pulchra*, the all-beautiful, for in her the radiance of God's glory shines forth'.[17] It is not of course clear that the Anglican members of ARCIC would necessarily subscribe to this particular eucharistic 'reading' of Mary. And other, fully humanly inclusive readings of sacramental theology and ecclesiology are possible and arguably necessary implications of reflection on 'Mary', as we shall see. In any case there is a serious question to be asked about the tendency in present-day theology to implode the meaning of 'sacrament' into 'eucharist' which does not self-evidently follow from reflection on Mary, unless her life is given a narrowly Christological reading.

To return to the contentious matter of definitions concerned with Mary it is interesting to notice that ARCIC tackles the dogma of the Immaculate Conception of Mary after discussion of her Assumption, and this is important, indicating that the latter does not depend on the former. It is at least arguable that here again 'the eschatological perspective illuminates our understanding of Mary's person and calling' (para. 59),[18] with divine grace filling her life from its beginning. We cannot at this juncture discuss the matter of how or whether this particular dogma could be received or 're-received' by Roman Catholics themselves, by members of the Church of England or the Anglican Communion, or in this particular case, by the Orthodox.[19] More constructive is attention to an essay by Rowan Williams, published when he was Bishop of Monmouth, which may ease matters somewhat. For Williams it is Mary's relation to the complete humanity of Jesus which is of particular importance here. Rightly he claims that what Jesus, 'humanly speaking', grew up into was made possible by his closest human contacts, that is, by those who first nurtured him. If he is indeed able to live in such a way that 'all his dealings are, without obstacle, open to God' this is enabled by what is given to him by the first human other he encounters. 'And that first human other is Mary.' His relations with both of his parents are at the foundation of his humanity, but 'more particularly, with Mary; hers is the first human face he will in any real sense be aware of. What he sees there is crucial to how he sees God'.[20] Without endorsing the doctrine of her Immaculate Conception, Williams finds the instinct behind the doctrine to be intelligible enough: 'Mary so lives in relation to God and others — including her son — that she makes her son uniquely free for God and for others'.[21] Her role is not only 'free consent' at the Annunciation, but it is 'all the diverse ways in which her freedom makes room for God throughout her life, in such a way that this freedom makes possible the humanity of her son'.[22] She enables in him 'a humanity in which there is no obstacle for the divine to be active and self-expressive'.[23] She receives 'the creative act of the Word before her work begins' of the formation of Jesus' human identity over time.[24] There is an emphasis too on 'the utter darkness' of her faith, 'so complete is her will to say yes to nothing but God'.[25]

We may recall at this point and juxtapose with Williams's reflections Cornelius Ernst's comment that 'Grace is not faceless',[26] which we may bear in mind for further reflections; but important too is Williams's understanding of the inter-dependence of human persons on one another, as well as his emphasis on Mary's free consent, her freedom. Whilst we may appreciate the determination of some theologians to dislodge all traces of pride and self-assertion from our understanding of Mary's assent[27] we have no need, if we are even to begin to understand her son, to turn her into some kind of doormat. To take the point about her free consent first, the ARCIC document does indeed refer to her 'free and unqualified consent in utter self-giving and trust' (para. 11)[28] — which we can illuminate by Williams's comment on 'the utter darkness of her faith' — but right from the introduction there is consistent reference to her as 'an exemplar of faithful obedience', paraphrased as 'the grace-filled response each of us is called to make to God, both personally and communally as the Church'.[29] We learn also that her response was not made 'without profound questioning', and that it issued 'in a life of joy intermingled with sorrow' (para. 5).[30] Obedience is consistently mentioned, as in for example the description of Mary as 'a model of holiness, obedience, and faith for all Chris tians' (para. 2)[31]; and virginity is understood not only as physical integrity but as 'an interior disposition of openness, obedience, and single-hearted fidelity' (para. 37).[32] Mary, we are informed, 'receives the angel's message and responds in humble obedience', one who represents 'the inwardness of faith and suffering' (para. 14).[33] No chance here of considering the possibility of Mary's response to God being one of delight, courage and generosity, which might produce an understanding of fruits of the Spirit' other than those being commended in the document. Nor, may we add, has obedience ever been identified as either a cardinal or theological virtue. And so far as understanding her son is concerned, it was C. S. Lewis, no less, who wrote that 'There is a fierceness, even a touch of Deborah, mixed with the sweetness in the *Magnificat* to which most painted Madonnas do little justice; matching the frequent severity of His own sayings', adding that one might suspect, 'on proper occasions, a certain astringency'.[34] Nor, within the scope of the verbal portrait of Mary emerging in the ARCIC document, is there room for interpretation of some of the struggles between mother and son which arguably are reflected in the New Testament texts,[35] with mother and family understandably fearing that Jesus' behaviour will have disastrous consequences for the whole group of his kin, and Mary in particular for a time being 'a living, critical, angry unadapted mother'.[36] Further, it would be too much to expect that the 'third quest' for the 'historical' Jesus would have much of an impact on the ARCIC document on Mary, though there is a reference to her as 'this Jewish woman of humble status, this daughter of Israel living in hope of justice for the poor' (para. 30),[37] which could be extended on the lines suggested by Jacob Neusner — Mary is akin to Rachel, whose relationship to God is such that her intervention may succeed when others fail.[38] With theologians of liberation, however, we need not simply 'tenderness and compassion' (para. 71),[39] but the defiant energy to refuse evil and work for a transformed world.[40] Whether it is the mothers and grandmothers of Argentina still seeking for their 'disappeared' ones, the abysmal maternal and infant mortality rates in so-called 'developing' countries, or the harrowing recollections of massacre,[41] joy joined with justice and peace (para. 74),[42] needs clearly to be 'angry and unadapted' and tough enough to refuse the perpetration of such horrors.

One major theologian who has indeed attempted to attend to new knowledge about what it would be like to be a first-century Jewish woman is Elizabeth Johnson, a major ecumenist and systematic theologian, and it is important that her work on Mary is part and parcel of a wider theological agenda.[43] She has the singular advantage of following on from the pioneering work of, for example, Rosemary Radford Ruether and Mary Daly in their different relationship to the Roman Catholic tradition on 'Mary'.[44] She is appropriately sensitive as a theologian who is a 'religious', not only to language which arguably contributes to the devaluation of women as co-procreators and co-nurturers of human life, but to the living of celibacy as fulfilment, lively aspiration and appropriate 'self-responsibility' in freedom — elements of the significance of 'virginity' lacking in the ARCIC document even when it refers to 'radical commitment to God' (para. 74).[45] She has argued eloquently that theologians must overcome the deep unease in the theology we have inherited about the association of the female and the feminine with the godlike such that divine transcendence is somehow compromised by such association, which in turn 'genderizes' ways of thinking, experiencing and expressing divine presence and immanence, sacramental or otherwise.

So one of her rules of thumb, as it were, follows from the principle that God transcends both sex and gender and from the principle that 'the unassumed is the unhealed', that is, that women are fully and completely human persons who are embraced by divine redemption. The theological rule of thumb with which we must then work is that the female-and-feminine can of and by itself image God in as full and in as limited a way as God is imaged by the male-and-masculine. Almost needless to add, remarkably little critical attention has been given in theology to what range of reference is included in the latter pair of terms.[46] As we have already seen in the ARCIC document on 'Mary', there are inbuilt and uncriticized assumptions about what is appropriate to the female/feminine well in evidence, though no doubt the defence would be offered that this is meant to be humanly inclusive—a defence which will not stand much critical examination if one attends to theological gender-constructions. One question that inevitably arises from Johnson's work is whether attention to the theological symbolization of 'Mary' inevitably detracts from attention to the humanly inclusive ways in which we do or do not 'image' God, and more particularly, whether such symbolization has to do with the alleged failure of western Christianity to overcome a defective doctrine of the Holy Spirit. There is a serious question here as to whether a great deal said of 'Mary' should more properly be referred to the Divine Spirit, with possibly significant consequences for the gender-constructions associated with some forms of ecclesiology.

Beyond some of the issues raised by the publication of *She Who Is* (1992), another of Professor Johnson's major publications has been *Friends of God and Prophets* (1998), remarkable for its ecumenical sensitivity, given that its author draws on a variety of insights from non-Roman Catholic traditions. The latter book is important for *Truly Our Sister* (2003),[47] quite apart from being germane to some of the issues raised in the ARCIC document and offering scope for discussion of the eschatological horizon of the last part of the Apostles' Creed. In *Truly Our Sister*, Professor Johnson suggests that she is proposing just one fruitful approach to the theology of Mary, seeking 'to understand her meaning as a particular person with her own life to compose'.[48] Whilst Professor Johnson acknowledges the ambiguity of traditions about Mary in affirming women's dignity, she wants to make a case for saying that 'the living remembrance of this woman can function positively to inspire the struggle for God's compassionate and liberating justice'.[49] Living in what she calls the 'post-industrial mainstream'[50] she wants to sound the challenge of discipleship afresh, but finds all too many features of the Marian tradition inhibiting that challenge, damaging the church's mission and the very possibility of transformative action. For her, the legacy of the Marian tradition can be dire, idealizing Mary to the detriment of other women, commending her holiness in such a way as to inculcate their subservience, and thereby their sociological subordination in both church and society. The ARCIC document merely says that the witness of Mary's 'obedience and acceptance of God's will has sometimes been used to encourage passivity and impose servitude on women' (para. 74),[51] and prefers therefore 'radical commitment to God', which is true as far as it goes, but hardly represents the problem of the legacy of the

Marian tradition for both women and men. For men may and do come
to revere Mary whilst ignoring or dominating the women around them,
whilst women find difficulty in claiming significant involvement in non-
domestic life, and access to the resources they and their families need in
order not merely to survive but to flourish. However, since churches as
compared with other organisations are the least likely to be open to the
authoritative participation of women, much the same phenomena can be
observed and experienced in ecclesial groups devoid of Marian tradition.
Habitable ecclesial abodes with or without Mary may not be readily
available, even if one follows the path recommended by Professor Johnson
here. For she identifies paths to be avoided, including dead-ends, searches
for earlier precedents, and then ventures her own proposals. These involve
picturing the world which the historical Mary inhabited. This results in
seeing her as a tough peasant woman, and in the light of this historical
realism Johnson puts together a mosaic from thirteen passages of Scripture
which situate Mary among the 'cloud of witnesses'. In other words, Mary is
taken off the pedestal on which she has been immobilized and re-joined
with the community of grace and struggle in history. No longer separated
from the rest of the 'splendid nobodies' who make up the majority of the
communion of saints, or hopelessly idealized, or given a life story in which
she is submissive, desexualized and fixated on the mothering of one male
child, much can be said by drawing on what we now know of the context in
which she lived and died, from archaeology, historical-critical and literary
study of texts, social sciences and comparative anthropology.

Picturing her world reconstrues Mary at the centre of a large brood of
children, one of whom was Jesus, central with her husband to an economic
group for whom the production of food and clothing was an unalterable
priority. Mary's religious life would flower in village assemblies, oral
communication of Torah to everyone, the practice of daily prayer, the weekly
Sabbath and the round of festivals. The portrait that emerges is refreshing
and stimulating, with Mary tethered into a world of historical specificity, a
woman who has a 'bodily, psychological, social relationship to the Messiah',[52]
and a sometimes agonizing life, if we compare her historical reality as a
person who received the news back in her own village of the death of this
son by state execution[53] with the exegesis of John 19 in which she appears
as paradigmatic disciple and witness, linking the significance of Jesus' death
with the gift of the Spirit and the foundation of a new community.[54] On
Professor Johnson's reading, remembrance here means a memory of grief to
galvanize non-violent action to stop violence and intimidation, rather than

a narrative symbolization of divine triumph which removes her from the lives of those who experience real horror (cf. 2 Maccabees 7 and the mother of the Maccabean martyrs). Beyond John 19, however, lie the possibilities implicit in Acts 2:17-18, given the presence of women there and then, and hence at the scene at Pentecost, Acts 1:14, with Mary explicitly mentioned (ARCIC para. 21),[55] Mary among women at this Spirit-giving foundation of the church.[56] From the earliest representations of Pentecost in the Rabbula Gospels (586 AD, from the monastery of St John of Zagba in Syria) Mary has been rightly placed at the heart of the group of the disciples, whilst it has been difficult, to put it mildly, to think that Mary's discipleship could have included the active proclamation of divine defeat of evil, in a mission comparable to those surrounding her at Pentecost.[57] If Mary is indeed to be continually relevant through the 'dynamic of prayer', as Professor Johnson proposes, however, it might well be that she could and indeed must be recoverable as the Spirit-graced, re-created Mary of the Assumption as one mediation of divine presence, with implications for the ministry of women and therefore of men in the church, and a renewed theology of sacrament and sacramentality, including that of 'Word', even though at present the stripping of one element of the theological scene is necessary. It would not be for the first time that to remedy one nest of problems, something possibly indispensable has to be left to one side for the time being until a moment for its recovery is ripe. If the overriding priority is the association of the female-and-feminine with the mystery of God, however, the symbolization of 'Mary' may block all routes to envisaging the divine in gender-inclusive ways, and if so, dismantling the 'sentimentalized Arianism' (my phrase, not Professor Johnson's) of that symbolization is essential, whilst the active recollection of Mary as an historical person must be recovered and remain.

Professor Johnson's proposals and conclusions were available in outline before the work was done which produced the ARCIC document, but they fall into the category of proposals actually generated from within the Christian tradition yet deemed not to be part of the tradition to which the drafters must seriously attend. It is obvious that Christian theological feminism simply has not yet been taken into the theological bloodstream of those likely to produce an acceptably ecumenical statement, although this ignores substantial and responsible criticism of the Christian tradition by feminist theologians, men as well as women, for over half a century.

If *Truly Our Sister* contains contentious proposals by prioritizing historicity rather than symbolization, Professor Tina Beattie's *God's Mother, Eve's Advocate* (2002) is even more so, in attending to symbolization. Her overall contention has to do with the place of female 'bodiliness' in the Christian story of salvation. She wants to avoid the fragmentation of the symbolization associated with Mary on the one hand, whilst arguing for its modification rather than its ossification on the other, by exposing the strategies which obliterate, conceal, displace or repress the significance of women's sexual difference from men and their distinctive identity. So whereas the church's earliest theologians used the insights of their own times and places to clarify and criticize their theological convictions, Professor Beattie deploys contemporary intellectual tools as she seeks change in theology of our own times, juxtaposing the old and new, the familiar and novel to achieve those changes. And she is right to stress that it is in liturgical performance that bodily expression is given to the language of faith, and that a major problem with the Marian tradition is that it requires only one such bodily expression, that of Mary as virginal mother, integrally connected as this is to the representation of the church as both bridal and maternal. Whereas both 'bride' and 'mother' are collective symbols, as 'holiness' was in the past in the sense that 'masculinity' was metaphor for spiritual progress for both sexes, the female-and-feminine is actually made redundant in the church's liturgical and bodily expression of redemption.

It is not possible here to do justice to the complexities of her position, but a central element in Professor Beattie's case could be used constructively and to correct the all too familiar Eve-Mary typology evident in the ARCIC document. In the document Mary is referred to as 'Eve's counterpart' (para. 35),[58] with reference to the contrast between Eve's disobedience resulting in death, but Mary's obedience opening the way to salvation (para. 36).[59] Professor Beattie picks up a phrase of Irenaeus in referring to Mary as Eve's advocate,[60] so for her it becomes Mary as it were 'voicing' Eve in the *Magnificat*,[61] bearing Eve in her own person, each implying the other. The ARCIC document writes, 'Hearing Eve called "the mother of all living" (Genesis 3:20), they may come to see Mary as mother of the new humanity, active in her ministry of pointing all people to Christ, seeking the welfare of all the living' (ARCIC, para. 72).[62] In the light of Beattie we could propose that Mary be recognized as mother of the new humanity because she stands not as counterpart to a disobedient Eve (all women other than Mary) but because Eve's 'mothering' of all living, graced by God, underlies and finds new embodiment in Mary, who speaks with her and for her. Eve and Mary then may be presented and re-presented in the living presence of women in the liturgy of the church, rather than Mary excluding them. This would indeed make it clear that as Mary 'received the Word in her heart and in her body, and brought it forth into the world' (ARCIC para. 51),[63] so, analogously, 'all ministries of the Church, especially those of Word and sacrament, mediate the grace of God through human beings' (para. 68),[64] which would mean, at last, women as well as men, women's bodily presence in the manifestation of salvation.

Whatever we think of the variety of proposals to which attention has been given here, it should at least be clear that 'Mary' not only has a continued 'life' in theological reflection, but that it is inexcusable for academic theological agendas to fail to attend to the Marian tradition, in which so many theological issues of central importance to the continued vitality of the Christian tradition find a particular expression.

NOTES TO CHAPTER 4

[1] Anglican-Roman Catholic International Commission (ARCIC), *Mary: Grace and Hope in Christ* (London: Morehouse, 2005), para. 7, p. 9.

[2] ARCIC, *Mary*, para. 7, p. 8.

[3] ARCIC, *Mary*, para 8., pp. 8-9.

[4] The ARCIC statement is referred to above by paragraph numbers. The statement with study guide is to be found in Donald Bolen and Gregory Cameron, eds, *Mary: Grace and Hope in Christ* (London: Continuum, 2006). For discussion see the Church of England Faith and Order Advisory Group, *Mary: Grace and Hope in Christ (ARCIC II, General Synod Misc. 872)* (London: Church House Publishing, 2006) and Mark E. Chapman, 'The Virgin Mary, Luther and the Church: A Doctrinal Interpretation from the Lutheran Perspective', *Ecumenical Trends* 36 (2007): 10-15. As Chapman points out in his first footnote (p. 15), the historical-critical method does not provide the doctrinal norm for all Lutheran biblical interpretation, and the Lutheran position is not 'dismissive of any doctrinal role of Mary'—a point unresolved and probably unresolvable in the Church of England. Excellent essays relevant to the discussion may be found in Sarah J. Boss, ed., *Mary: The Complete Resource* (London: Continuum, 2007).

[5] ARCIC, *Mary*, pp. 49-55.

[6] ARCIC, *Mary*, p. 50.

[7] The 'Dormition' or 'falling asleep' of Mary is celebrated in Orthodox churches on 15th August, as is the 'Assumption' of Mary, defined by the then Pope in 1950 as a dogma which Roman Catholics are bound to believe. The dogma makes a theological claim which is 'infallibly' defined, and both definition and 'infallibility' remain matters of contention between the Orthodox and the Roman Catholic Church, as well as between Protestants and Roman Catholics.

[8] ARCIC, *Mary*, p. 8.

[9] ARCIC, *Mary*, p. 55, note 10.

[10] August 15 (traditionally the Feast of the Assumption) has recently been restored to the Calendar of the Church of England simply as a feast for 'The Blessed Virgin Mary'. It had survived in the Calendar of Oxford University, and had in any case (sometimes as the 'Dormition') appeared long since in the Prayer Books of many Anglican churches world-wide. It is a pity, however, that the 'epistle of the Old Testament' once associated with the feast, from Ecclesiasticus 24 has not been restored as a reading (on Anglican tradition, see Ann Loades, 'The Position of the Anglican Communion Regarding the Trinity and Mary', *New Blackfriars* 82 [2001]: 364-74). In the ARCIC document itself, although the covenant between God and Israel is several times described as a 'love affair' and 'nuptial imagery' is also used in the New Testament to describe the relationship between Christ and the Church (para 9, pp. 10-11) there is no reference to the Song of Songs and all the imagery associated with it, both verbal and visual. As Martin Warner has pointed out, this is arguably a significant lack in the ARCIC document (see Martin Warner, 'Mary: Grace and Hope in Christ: A New Understanding of Scripture and Tradition?', *International Journal for the Study of the Christian Church* 5 (2005): 265-71. And, we may add, most certainly in the current authorized Church of England liturgy for August 15. Only at para 13 (p. 14) is there explicit reference to 'the Christian imagination' though the document depends upon it as it veers from considering Mary as an historical figure to considering her as a symbolic figure. See the classic discussion of the differences in Elizabeth A. Johnson, 'The Symbolic Character of Statements about Mary', *Journal of Ecumenical Studies* 22 (1985): 312-35.

[11] See Loades, 'The Position', p. 374.

[12] ARCIC, *Mary*, p. 25.

[13] ARCIC, *Mary*, p. x.

[14] ARCIC, *Mary*, p. 68.

[15] ARCIC, *Mary*, pp. 65-66.

[16] Benedict XVI, Sacramentum caritatis. *Postsynodical Exhortation on the Eucharist of the Holy Father Benedict XVI to the Bishops, Clergy, Consecrated Persons and the Lay Faithful on the Eucharist as the Source and Summit of the Church's Life and Mission* (London: Catholic Truth Society, 2007).

[17] It is worth attending to the cover picture of the Catholic Truth Society edition, with the Pope administering the eucharist to a woman religious. Cf. Edward Schillebeeckx, *Mary, Mother of the Redemption: The Religious Basis of the Mystery of Mary* (London: Sheed and Ward, 1964), p. 172: 'It is clear that she must be a creature of matchless wonder, this *Immaculata* and *Assumpta*, with whom even the most physically and spiritually beautiful woman in the world cannot in anyway be compared'. See Ann Loades, 'The Virgin Mary and the Feminist Quest', in Janet Martin Soskice, ed., *After Eve* (London: Collins, 1990), pp. 156-178 and Ann Loades, 'Feminist Theology: A View of Mary', in William McLoughlin and Jill Pinnock, eds, *Mary is for Everyone: Essays on Mary and Ecumenism* (Leonminster: Gracewing, 1997), pp. 32-40, for discussion of some other recent generous papal statements.

[18] ARCIC, *Mary*, p. 57.

[19] See the proposals for Protestants in George Lindbeck, *The Nature of Doctrine: Religion and Theology in a Post-liberal Age* (Louisville, Kenn.: Westminster John Knox, 1984), pp. 96-98.

[20] Rowan Williams, '"The Seal of Orthodoxy": Mary and the Heart of Christian Doctrine', in Martin Warner, ed., *Say Yes to God: Mary and the Revealing of the Word Made Flesh* (London: Tufton, 1999), pp. 15-29, at p. 19.

[21] Williams, 'Seal of Orthodoxy', pp. 19-20.

[22] Williams, 'Seal of Orthodoxy', p. 20.

[23] Williams, 'Seal of Orthodoxy', p. 21.

[24] Williams, 'Seal of Orthodoxy', p. 22.

[25] Williams, 'Seal of Orthodoxy', p. 27.

[26] Cornelius Ernst, *Multiple Echo* (London: Darton, Longman and Todd, 1979), p. 124.

[27] Jan Miric Lochmann, *The Faith We Confess: An Ecumenical Dogmatics* (Philadelphia, Penn.: Fortress Press, 1984), pp. 112-13.

[28] ARCIC, *Mary*, p. 13.

[29] ARCIC, *Mary*, p. x.

[30] ARCIC, *Mary*, p. 7.

[31] ARCIC, *Mary*, p. 3.

[32] ARCIC, *Mary*, p. 34.

[33] ARCIC, *Mary*, p. 15.

[34] C. S. Lewis, *Reflections on the Psalms* (London: Fontana, 1961), p. 13.

[35] John Macquarrie, *Mary for All Christians* (Edinburgh: T and T Clark, 2001), pp. 35-40.

[36] Elisabeth Moltmann-Wendel, *A Land Flowing with Milk and Honey* (London: SCM Press, 1986), pp. 193-95.

[37] ARCIC, *Mary*, p. 28.

[38] Jacob Nuesner, 'Can Judaism Make Any Sense of Christianity? The Case of Mary as Mother of God', in his *Jews and Christians: The Myth of a Common Tradition* (London: SCM Press, 1991), pp. 117-29, p. 127.

[39] ARCIC, *Mary*, p. 71.

[40] Ivone Gebara and Maria Clara Bingemer, *Mary: Mother of God, Mother of the Poor* (London: Burns and Oates, 1989).

[41] Antonia Arslan, *Skylark Farm* (London: Atlantic, 2008).

[42] ARCIC, *Mary*, p. 74.

[43] Elizabeth A. Johnson, *She Who Is: The Mystery of God in Feminist Discourse* (New York, N.Y.: Crossroad, 1992).

[44] Loades, 'Feminist Quest'.

[45] ARCIC, *Mary*, p. 74.

[46] Richard H. Roberts, 'Man/Masculinity', in Adrian Hastings, ed., *The Oxford Companion to Christian Thought* (Oxford: Oxford University Press, 2000), pp. 404-6.
[47] Elizabeth A. Johnson, *Truly Our Sister: A Theology of Mary in the Communion of Saints* (London: Continuum, 2003), pp. 305-25.
[48] Johnson, *Truly Our Sister*, pp. xiii-xiv.
[49] Johnson, *Truly Our Sister*, p. xiv.
[50] Johnson, *Truly Our Sister*, p. xv.
[51] ARCIC, *Mary*, p. 74.
[52] Johnson, *Truly Our Sister*, p. 314.
[53] Johnson, *Truly Our Sister*, pp. 293-97.
[54] John McHugh, 'Behold Your Mother: Reflections on John 19.25-27', in William McLoughlin and Jill Pinnock, eds, *Mary is For Everyone: Essays on Mary and Ecumenism* (Leominster: Gracewing, 1997); ARCIC, *Mary*, pp. 21-26 (paras 22-27).
[55] ARCIC, Mary, p. 21.
[56] Johnson, *Truly Our Sister*, pp. 297-304; cf. also Anthony J. Tambasco, *What are They Saying about Mary?* (Mahwah, N.J.: Paulist Press, 1984), pp. 73-83.
[57] For example, Richard Cross, 'On the Polity of God: The Ecclesiology of Duns Scotus', *International Journal for the Study of the Christian Church* 7 (2007): 29-45, at p. 44, note 68.
[58] ARCIC, *Mary*, p. 33.
[59] ARCIC, *Mary*, pp. 33-4.
[60] Irenaeus, *Against Heresies* 5.19.1.
[61] Tina Beattie, *God's Mother, Eve's Advocate: A Marian Narrative of Women's Salvation* (London: Continuum, 2000), p. 126.
[62] ARCIC, *Mary*, p. 72.
[63] ARCIC, *Mary*, p. 48.
[64] ARCIC, *Mary*, p. 68.

5

The Nativity in Recent Poetry

Both 'poetry' and 'prose' (as forms of 'poiesis') can stretch the resources of human language to their limits when we try to say things of which we can hardly speak or write. This may especially be the case when some understanding of the matter in hand is of the greatest importance to us. In the case of the nativity, we are concerned with one central truth, that God's Son (Jesus of Nazareth) 'was incarnate of the Holy Spirit and the Virgin Mary'. As Les Murray puts it, God can be regarded as the 'poetry caught' (but not trapped) within a religious tradition, and poetry, for Murray, offers the opportunity of 'whole thinking'.[1]

We can also attend to Elizabeth Jennings' remarks when reviewing a book by a Dominican theologian, Thomas Gilby. There she affirms that he had given poetry 'a central and high place in human experience', for its 'moments of revelation' involve the whole of a person 'transcribing or responding to the most important function of life-knowing by loving and loving by knowing', grasping an experience 'not to possess but to be possessed'.[2]

The fact that a poet is attending to and expressing a central truth of religion, however, never excuses anything other than one's best work, which will include technical skill and rhythmical dexterity, though even more important are seriousness of purpose and intensity of feeling.[3]

Jennings goes on to assert that a specifically Christian poet, writing on a central truth such as that of the Incarnation, must never cease to care, and be prepared to struggle through her task, alert to the experiments and changes of the age in which she finds herself.

Since the seventeenth century, in particular, the poet writes not so much for the public context of worship, but to articulate personal experience of truth. Moreover, not only does the poem indeed spring from the whole person, but a specifically Christian poet readily acknowledges that her 'making' is 'a small participation in the divine and unceasing act of creation'—whether everyone recognizes this or not.[4]

And she assesses what is happening in the making of poetry in the broadest sense—which we may take to be true of the biblical poets too—when she reflects that

> the first vivid vision is bound to fade a little when words intervene. On the other hand, how can a man or woman know what they have experienced until they try to speak about it? Poetry would certainly seem to be the most suitable medium for such explanations.[5]

Despite these observations, it does not follow that poets will be free from doubt and difficulties in regard either to their work or to their faith. On the contrary, the more perceptive one is, the more agonized one might feel about the way things in life seem to go and the relationship of God to it all.

Biblical poetry

When we turn to the biblical poets of the nativity, we need to reflect on more than the first few chapters of the Gospels of Matthew and Luke if we are to begin to be able to grasp their distinctive poetry as they grappled with the astonishing claims made by early Christianity. As the Christian tradition developed, the Roman winter solstice celebrations were displaced by celebrations of Jesus' birth, quite likely in the fourth century of the Christian era. The imperial Sun of Victory was displaced by the celebration of a divine and human Son, whose victory was profoundly different in what it offered to the hopes and longings of human beings.

One major text of great importance for expressing Christian convictions—read out loud, chanted, and learned by heart—was the Book of Isaiah.[6]

The prophet who gave the whole book its name was deemed to have foreseen the arrival of the anointed one, the Messiah, the Christ, someone of special importance as the sign of God's presence with and among humankind (Isa. 7:14). The original prophet had addressed a message to his king, Ahaz, in the besieged city of Jerusalem, promising that by the time a young woman—probably Ahaz's wife—had conceived and borne a son (Immanuel), the city would be free of its enemies. By the time of the birth of Jesus, these words were known both to Hebrew- and to Greek-speaking hearers and readers of Scripture.[7]

Picked up by the writer of the first Gospel (Matt.1:23), they interpreted the meaning of the message given to Joseph by an angel, in a dream about the significance of the child to be born to Mary. The writer was simply continuing what seems likely to have been the tradition of Christians since well before his own time, that of finding in their Scriptures, shared with Jewish friends and neighbours and fellow-worshippers, the language by which he and others could express and interpret what was going on in the nativity. And as early as the second century, a representation of Isaiah was to be found in a wall painting near to an image of Mary with her child on her lap—Christ sprung from the root of Jesse—with Isaiah pointing to them.[8] In this painting Isaiah also points to a star near them, the 'star out of Jacob' (Num. 24:17), the star of Matthew's second chapter that guides the mysterious magi on their way (Matt.2:2).

So, Isaiah the prophet was also seen as Isaiah the evangelist, with some two hundred and fifty quotations from or allusions to the Book of Isaiah in Christian Scriptures, from Matthew to Revelation. It later even became a tradition to write up the whole narrative of Christ's life and its meaning, from Nativity to Last Judgment, in the very language of Isaiah.[9]

It was as though, having grasped the significance of Christ in connection with the promise of salvation so characteristic of the Book of Isaiah, Christians could use poetry already familiar in order to retell the meaning of the Incarnation. It may even be the case that the poetry of Isaiah formed both Mary's own understanding of her role in bringing the divine presence among humanity in an unprecedented way, and then formed Jesus' own struggle to understand his relationship to God, his mission and death, and even perhaps God-given resurrection (see Isa 25:7-8).

The Book of Isaiah contains the words of a poet of the most profound insight and the most extraordinary expectations. For he spoke also of a multitude of camels corning from Midian, Ephah, and Sheba, bearing gold and frankincense, proclaiming the praise of the Lord (Isa 60:6). It was like the kings spoken of by the Psalmist, with kings of Tarshish, Sheba, and Seba rendering tribute (Ps 72:10-11). In Isaiah they are, as it were, silenced by what they come to see in Christ: 'Kings shall shut their mouths because of him; for that which has not been told them they shall see, and that which they have not heard they shall understand' (Isa 52:15). And there was the exultant praise of God to be found later in Isaiah, where the poet writes of being clothed with 'garments of salvation' and 'the robe of righteousness', like a groom and bride adorned for their marriage: 'For as the earth brings forth its shoots, and as a garden causes what is sown in it to spring up, so the Lord God will cause righteousness and praise to spring forth before all the nations' (Isa 61:10-11).[10]

Moreover, Isaiah acknowledged the created context in which human beings are set, not only with his vision of the holy mountain and its restored and paradisal state (Isa 11:6-9), but also remembering and recalling how interdependent human beings remain with their animal companions and workmates, naming specifically the ox and ass as beasts of burden indeed, but capable of knowing their owner and stable (Isa 1:3). Long after Christian Scriptures had been identified and agreed as authoritative, these animal companions turned up in paintings, dramatic representations, and inevitably, in poetry. In addition, because Luke's Gospel brings shepherds to Jesus' birthplace there might be lambs too, in all their shivering vulnerability, associated so closely with the infant that they may symbolize him.[11]

Mother, father, and God

We can keep other biblical texts in mind too before we turn to the poetry concerned with the nativity, poetry that is very much of our own era. Of central importance was something shared with most human beings about the significance of children to families and their networks of kin. Indeed, children have been especially significant when the divine blessing of fertility was jeopardized in poor communities by inadequate food and scarcity of resources, and inevitably untreated and untreatable infections in those of uncertain health. If we attend to the high mortality rate for both women and newborns in all but the most privileged societies, we can refresh our sensitivity not only to the way in which divine creativity was deemed to be present in the 'genesis' and growth of the child in her or his mother's womb (for example, Job 10:10; Ps 139:13-16; Ps 22:9-10—from the Psalm attributed to Christ in his last agony), but also to the point that a child's being brought safely through birth, and being nurtured and reared, yielded insight into God's own compassion (Isa 42:14; 46:3-4).

The relationship between the nascent and born child and mother is surely the primary model of altruism and intra-dependence in human societies. In scriptural texts, it is also the primary model for the cooperation of divine grace and human well-being as expressed in fertility. There were children born blind, deaf, mute, or otherwise disabled, but none of the risks either to mother or to child destroyed this conviction. Being safely born to the one whose heartbeat had been known before birth, able to breathe and suckle, being given to one's mother to feed and nurture, just able to focus eyes to eyes on her loving, smiling, singing, and talking face, learning to sing-along, being cleaned up, kept safe enough, seen through being sick, sleepless, runny-nosed, disruptive, demanding, and impossible to please (just like an adult!), eager, curious, enjoying play of all kinds, making things for fun, learning companionship and conviviality in the sharing of food, learning how to let go of hurts and harms so that life could go on- all this might be involved as a child grew into the 'image of God', as well as becoming of an age to learn Scripture by heart and sing it to others. Moreover, it is no accident that images of a breastfeeding maternal figure are so central in human art, not least in Christian art and poetry, since if a child's birth-mother could not feed him or her, or if she died, the child's very life depended upon another woman being able and willing to do so. Hence it remains a central image of human and divine charity.

Important too is the father's role. Being a 'father'—as even the unnameable but awesomely named 'Adonai' could sometimes be addressed (Isa 63:16)—had to do with creativity, intimacy, and hope, and above all with the understanding that Adonai was self-revealed as mercy (Exod 3:14; 34:6). So, we need to keep Joseph in mind, and arguably give him far more attention than has been commonly the case, despite the efforts of some from the seventeenth century onward. Whatever may have been taken for granted in biblical or other times and places about a father's presence in his family, it cannot always be so taken for granted today. And it would be easy to break a man's heart if he thought that the one to whom he was betrothed had been unfaithful to him. So, if Joseph is to embody in his own distinctive way the divine compassion, both to a vulnerable young woman and to the child she bears, he needs that promise from Isaiah.[12]

As is now widely appreciated, Matthew's Gospel genealogy associates Jesus with some vulnerable, marginal, possibly scandalous, and indeed unconventional women, but Joseph, we may suppose, had never thought himself likely to be involved with one such.[13] So his consent to Mary's well-being and that of her child is crucial for their gift of life to the community in which they will live, every birth bringing with it the promise of new beginnings. It was not just one more mouth to feed. We might well think that there is an untapped vein of reflection here, not least for poets of our own time, and for societies where a 'parent' may not be genetically related to a child but be a good parent nonetheless, and where all adults care for and respect one another's children.

So far as Joseph himself is concerned, and what Jesus may have learned from him about the divine 'fatherhood', one of the most illuminating comments comes not from a poet but from someone concerned precisely with the fate of children in our own societies. As Alice Miller says, even someone who assumes that Jesus owed his capacity to love, his authenticity, and his goodness to the grace of his divine father may well wonder why God entrusted Jesus to these particular parents.[14] It makes more sense, however, generously to think of Joseph also being graced by God, and so to deepen our appreciation of the role of Joseph in Jesus' life, never calling attention to himself, protecting and loving Mary and the child, encouraging him, assigning him central importance, and serving him, doing his share of making it possible for the child to distinguish what was true and to experience the meaning of love.[15]

The consequences of Joseph's actions were to be of the greatest significance, as indicated in the conclusion to Pamela Vermes' poem, 'Think':

> Think that uniquely,
> in all the history of holiness,
> a man lived in the Presence,
> as a son with his father,
> walking hand in hand,
> speaking mouth to mouth.
> Think that uniquely,
> in all the history of holiness,
> a man said,
> with his life and death,
> Be a child
> as I am the child
> of our father in heaven.
> That the prophecy of Hosea might be fulfilled.
> That whereas it had been said of them,
> You are not my people, it might be said of them,
> CHILDREN OF THE LIVING GOD.[16]

At the very least we may say that it is not unfitting to attribute Jesus' extraordinary confidence in addressing God and listening for God, responding to God, to his experience of human fathering by Joseph. The child and other children valued by Joseph would be cherished by the community to which they belonged, with its care for one another through the generations. So his support (for as long as it was present) was central to Jesus' earthly life. However, Joseph's support does not seem to have lasted until Jesus reached adult standing, for Joseph—through death, presumably—disappears from the narrative of his son's life (see Mark 6:3).

Poetry, nativity, and context

As a result of entirely new studies, we may well have a much better comprehension of the world into which Jesus was born, and the place of his mother within her village society.[17] She would need to be tough enough to survive pregnancy and a safe birth, healthy enough to feed and nurture her child, while living as one of a group of adults of different generations, with a swarm of children, all as soon as they were able likely to be involved in securing food and clothing and shelter as an ever-urgent priority. Their religious life would take place in village assemblies, including the developing synagogue tradition, with oral teaching not only of Torah but of other Scriptures—including the Book of Isaiah, as has been suggested earlier. Daily prayer was part and parcel of life, as was Sabbath respite from back-breaking work, and a round of festivals. No one would readily draw upon themselves and their community the attention of the 'authorities', least of all the attention of the occupying power, which had no qualms about destroying opposition, polluting village wells with corpses, wrecking vineyards and fields, razing villages to the ground, crucifying the men, and turning women and children off to fend for themselves if they could - or else to die if they could not.

Whatever we make of Mary's relationship to Jesus while young, some of the personal differences between them of which we have glimpses in the Gospels (for example, Mark 3:31-35) may well have stemmed from her grasp of the fact that he put his kin at risk by his preaching and behaviour. Virtually none of this appears as yet in British poetry of our time, and generally there is little realism about Jesus' birth either.

Just occasionally someone risks the provocation of insisting on that realism—such as Guy Reid's tiny statue of Mary and her child to be found in St Matthew's Anglican Church, Westminster. Not only is Reid's 'Mary' no example of great physical beauty such as we associate with some of the greatest paintings of the past; she is also completely naked, and the child- equally naked, as had become familiar in art from the past, though here no advertisement for infant beauty—is perched very uneasily on his mother's knee.[18] So far as I am aware, this is the first representation of a fully naked Mary ever produced by a British artist, and it prompted outrage in some quarters—in a society in which female nudity or near-nudity is hardly unfamiliar in anything from 'lap-dancing' to advertising and fashion-wear (all of which may be part of the problem). The outrage nevertheless tells us something about our disquiet at the realism we need if we are to begin to grasp the enormity of the Christian claim about Incarnation. From this perspective, the poem by Alla Renee Bozarth has a powerful message:

> Before his cry,
> her cry.
> Before his sweat
> of blood,
> her bleeding and tears.
> Before his offering, hers.
> And by her body and blood
> alone, his body and blood
> and whole human being.[19]

It seems that we still have not reached the point where we can take such realism for granted, and in any event, it is little to the fore in the poetry discussed here. With or without such realism, the Christian claim about the truth of the Incarnation remains astonishing, as Denise Levertov points up in her poem 'On the Mystery of the Incarnation':

> It's when we face for a moment
> the worst our kind can do, and shudder to know
> the taint in our own selves, that awe
> cracks the mind's shell and enters the heart:
> not to a flower, not to a dolphin,
> to no innocent form
> but to this creature vainly sure
> it and no other is god-like, God
> (out of compassion for our ugly
> failure to evolve) entrusts,
> as guest, as brother,
> the Word.[20]

The Word, however, is not separated from the non-human creatures whose presence in the nativity scene (as it were) derives originally from Isaiah's visions—not forgetting the Greek version of the prophet Habakkuk, finding God's work between two animals.[21] The creatures on whom human beings so depend are represented (in Levertov's words) by 'the wondering animals unused to human company after dark' who witness the birth, hear the first cry 'of earthly breath drawn through the newborn lungs of God / and the cord is cut ...'. Before any other arrivals the ox and the ass are already kneeling, 'the Family's oldest friends'.[22]

Given our much greater sense of relationship to the non-human creatures with whom we share so much, it is unsurprising that poets of our time extend the friends of the family to include other creatures. Thus Les Murray's 'Animal Nativity' is integral to his collection 'Translations from the Natural World', and he writes that the great tale of peace started with the agreement of Mary ('this girl'). He then describes the flitting of swallows within the stable, as if another swallow is hatching and turning human. In the poet's vision, cattle are content that 'this calf' must come in human form, and spiders recognize someone else able to walk on water. Finally, Murray speaks of dogs witnessing the nativity scene—not the well-fed pets of our modern western culture, but 'starving' dogs, 'agog' at the presence of the newborn child.[23]

U. A. Fanthorpe indeed writes as it were from a sheepdog's perspective, the dog recalling the very bright light, 'the talking bird', the singing. 'And the sky filled up wi' wings / And then the silence'. The shepherds, 'our lads', use local dialect to tell the dog to stay with the sheep. They return and report back: what they had seen included camels and kings, with presents—'Not the kind you eat'—as well as a baby. 'Presents wes for him. / Our lads took him a lamb'.

> I had to stay behind wi't' sheep.
> Pity they didn't tek me along too.
> I'm good wi' lambs,
> And the baby might have liked a dog
> After all that myrrh and such.[24]

It does not seem that poems have yet been written from the perspective of the camels and dromedaries, however, perhaps because such animals are foreign to British circumstances, though vital in their relationship with the human beings to whose survival they contribute!

The cosmic context is maintained in two ways, we may think. One is by reference to the mystery of angelic presence: the strange, ambivalent creatures who serve as messengers on occasion, as well as overshadowing the throne of God, provide the divine being with a chariot of perplexing beauty and become warriors for justice. They are perhaps best appreciated, not in words, but rather via Olivier Messiaen's great musical meditation on the Nativity (his 1935 organ suite *La Nativité du Seigneur*), whose sixth section deals with the angels. Indeed he finds them as we do in biblical poetry. They matter not least because they remind us of the worship and celebration of God in which we may participate.

Perhaps more intelligible for us than angels is the significance attributed to the star, which as it were is inevitably associated with singing the magi through their travails of 'salt, snow, skulls'.[25] Most movingly, George Mackay Brown meditates on the 'Desert Rose' of Isa 35:1 (not the 'crocus' of modern translations), the rose without thorns traditionally taken as a reference to Mary. The travellers linger, stir the rose's incense, journey on, and the rose is left to suffer 'the barren gold of the sun', until a star lifts its head, murmurs to the rose, and "Midnight, the star throng, shed / Dew in my cup like wine".[26] Mackay Brown also imagines himself as a king, one of the magi watching the stars.

> What wandered about the star streets
> Last night, late?
> It knocked for shelter at doors of gold, like a lost boy.
> My heart was bruised with the image.
> I am waiting now at sunset, again, with my charts.
> I had perhaps drunk too much midnight wine.

> He sits at the window, and the stars identify themselves.

> I greet those faithful
> Who troop to my dark window.
> What should I say
> To this one, intruder and stranger?
> He has stood there two nights
> And is silent still.
> I imagine a title,
> 'Keeper of the Door of Corn'.
> And a word, 'Come'.[27]

David Gascoyne has reflected on the genesis of stars discerned by modern astronomy, and finds the star seemingly born of two others:

> unseen
> But shining everywhere
> The third star balanced shall henceforward burn
> Through all dark still to come, serene,
> Ubiquitous, immaculately clear;
> A magnet in the middle of the maze, to draw us on
> Towards that Bethlehem beyond despair
> Where from the womb of Nothing shall be born
> A Son.[28]

The star becomes not just the star of the magi, but a star for us, however mysterious the 'Nothing' of divine being. Like the writers of the Gospels, the poet enables us to make something of the event for ourselves.

Mary the Mother of Jesus

The Gospel writers, however, have above all to make something of the kind of person Mary, the mother of Jesus, must have been by the time of Jesus' conception, as well as what she was to become. Yet we know little of her as her own person, so to speak, from the glimpses we have of her in the Gospels, leading to her presence in the midst of Jesus' disciples in Acts 1:14 after his resurrection-recreation by God. It is important to keep in mind the trajectory of Spirit-presence to her at the beginning of Luke's Gospel through to the Spirit-presence to her and Jesus' disciples in the new community being formed in Acts. Grace and Spirit do not leave her, whatever her own struggles, as she too becomes a disciple of her son. The greeting of Gabriel to her acknowledges her as graced indeed, even before the conception of her son.

Yet we need a note of caution here, for some theologians have treated her as so entirely dependent on divine grace, dislodging any hint of human self-assertion from her response to Gabriel, that her personal human dignity is eliminated. Rather, we may regard her as indeed a profoundly graced person, so she can be thought of as bringing everything that she was as a life-giver to her response to Gabriel's challenge. She cannot be described as so subservient as to make unintelligible either her response to that or Jesus' own response to God. It is as though she recovers herself in the presence of the angel, no longer somewhat intimidated as she may well have been at first, for she takes the angel on in conversation. She may have considered the risks of being abandoned by Joseph, socially ostracized, dying in childbirth, or surviving but being vulnerable to threats both to herself and to her child, as indeed proved to be the case. Thus, writing on Botticelli's painting 'The Cestello Annunciation', Andrew Hudgins has the angel first crowding her and then responding to her backing away.

> He kneels. He's come in all unearthly innocence
> to tell her of glory-not knowing, not remembering
> how terrible it is. And Botticelli
> gives her eternity to turn, ...
> ... But her whole body pulls away.
> Only her head, already haloed, bows,

Acquiescing. And though she will, she's not yet said:
Behold, I am the handmaid of the Lord,
As Botticelli, in his great pity,
Lets her refuse, accept, refuse, and think again.[29]

Beyond her graced response to the awesome mystery into which she is drawn, Elizabeth Jennings pictures Mary sitting in ecstasy, now that the terrifying angel has left her:

> She can
> Take comfort from the things she knows
> Though in her heart new loving burns
> Something she never gave to man
>
> Or god before, and this god grows
> Most like a man. She wonders how
> To pray at all, what thanks to give
> And whom to give them to. 'Alone
> To all men's eyes I must now go'
> She thinks, 'And by myself must live
> With a strange child that is my own.'[30]

As it happens, she is not bereft of Joseph's continuing love for her and his support, but she had to consider the possibility in the first place. It hardly makes sense, therefore, to suppose that her ecstatically embracing God's designs for her is to become subservient in becoming 'handmaid'. It is surely a state of honour, not of subjection. And although Denise Levertov does not explicitly make the connection between learning to attain freefall 'and float / into Creator Spirit's deep embrace, knowing no effort earns / that allsurrounding graces'[31] and what she says of Mary, that connection can indeed be made. Mary in that embrace is a figure not of 'obedience'—which has never been understood to be a cardinal (let alone a theological) virtue in Christian tradition—but of great courage. Indeed, her *Magnificat* (Luke 1:46-55) insistently reminds us of her courage as she allies herself with the divine defeat of evil. She chooses fertility and life, not humiliation and pain, though that may inescapably follow.

In 'Annunciation' Denise Levertov indicates the kind of scene we may find in a painting, the furnishing of the room-including lectern and book, and 'always / the tall lily'.[32] The angelic ambassador arrives and is acknowledged as a guest.

> But we are told of meek obedience. No one mentions
> Courage.
> The engendering Spirit
> Did not enter her without consent.
> God waited.
> She was free
> to accept or to refuse, choice
> integral to humanness.

Levertov goes on to query annunciations of one sort or another in most of our lives. We may respond to these and act unwillingly, in sullen pride, uncomprehending, or turn away from them in dread, weakness, despair, or relief: 'Ordinary lives continue. / God does not smite them. / But the gates close, the pathway vanishes'. Mary had been much like others, except that she wept only for pity and laughed in joy: 'Compassion and intelligence / fused in her, indivisible'. She did not quail but attended gravely and courteously to what was being asked of her, in due time to

> push out into air, a Man-child
> needing, like any other,
> milk and love—
> but who was God.
> This was the minute no one speaks of,
> when she could still refuse.
> A breath unbreathed,
> Spirit,
> suspended,
> waiting.

However, she neither cried her unworthiness, nor appealed to her lack of strength. She neither submitted with gritted teeth, nor raged at being coerced.

> Bravest of all humans,
> consent illumined her
> The room filled with its light,
> the lily glowed in it,
> and the iridescent wings.
> Consent,

> courage unparalleled,
> opened her utterly.[33]

Furthermore, there is nothing in the biblical poetry of the scene that absolutely separates and distinguishes Mary from all other women in her graced and courageous consent to childbearing. Indeed, insofar as what is happening is an anticipation of a restored Eden, Mary needs to be allied with 'Eve (herself 'Mother of all living' in Gen 3:20) and not employed to denigrate 'Eve' and the multiple possibilities of women's lives—though we cannot say that this has been much addressed in theology of our time, let alone in poetry.[34] A new Eden is being found over again:

> The child
> holds out both his hands
> for the breast's apple. The snake is asleep.[35]

No snake poses a danger for the time being, but that does not protect the child from possible fears.

> This God fears the night,
> A child so terrified he asks for us.
> God is the cry we thought came from our own
> Perpetual sense of loss.
> Can God be frightened to be so alone?
> Does that child dream the Cross?[36]

In fact, he does not need to be thought of as so dreaming, whatever is to be made of his future significance. Rather, it might well be that he shares the familiar fears of childhood, fearing that the light will not return.

> The night comes up over you, faceless and forbidden,
> over the hawk sunk in earth and the sun drunk by the sea;
> and who can tell, the child said, no matter what they say—
> who can be sure that the sun will rise on another day?[37]

The light indeed returns, and for those who welcome the child, such as Simeon (commemorated at the Feast of Candlemas, the Feast of the Presentation), that certitude sustains them, however terrible life may become.[38] And the snake awakes in good time with 'Queen Herod protecting her own by urging the slaughter of other children.[39] Mary becomes another Rachel (Jer. 31:15), weeping and taken by Joseph fleeing into exile, but like Rachel who has the ear of God, able eventually to return to a future—though of a kind no one could have foreseen.

The poet H.D. [Hilda Doolittle] reflects on that future beyond the eventual tragedy and horror, linking in a most original fashion the gift of one of the magi with the different narratives of the gift of the woman who anoints Jesus' feet, his head, and finally comes to anoint his body. She buys her alabaster jar of ointment from Kasper, the name traditionally given to one of the three magi-turned-kings. In 'The Flowering of the Rod', H.D. reimagines the three magi coming to Jesus' birthplace, the ox-stall, with Balthasar and Melchior taking first and second place in their presentation of gifts to the child and making their appropriate reverence to the child and his mother.[40] Balthasar bows low, Melchior kisses the earth, but Kasper stands somewhat to one side, relatively unimportant, bowing his head slightly to indicate the almost negligible part he felt himself to be playing in the ritual of presentation. When she speaks, he looks toward her and sees her youthful shyness. She detects a 'most beautiful fragrance', seemingly from his jar, even though its seal is not yet broken. Kasper realizes that the aroma comes from the 'bundle of myrrh' that she is holding.

We observed earlier that we need to keep in mind the whole trajectory from Spirit-presence with Mary at the Annunciation to Spirit-presence after Jesus' having been raised by God to a transformed life and a new form of presence in human community. H.D. has already made this point in her inimitable way before she names Mary of Magdala or recounts her meeting with Kasper. Writing from the perspective of envisioning the recovered Paradise of human longing, she describes the resurrection as a 'bee-line' that goes directly to plunder the 'honeycomb' and bring the aroma of 'myrrh and balm'.[41] In the meantime, so to speak, we can invoke David Gascoyne for our last word, asking that God grant that we

> Give birth to the world's only Prince, *Puer Aeternus*, He
> Whose swordlike Word comes not to bring us peace but war
> Within forever against falsehood and all fratricidal War.[42]

NOTES TO CHAPTER 5

[1] Les Murray, 'Poetry and Religion', in *Collected Poems* (Manchester: Carcanet, 1998), p. 267.

[2] Elizabeth Jennings, *Every Changing Shape: Mystical Experience and the Making of Poems* (Manchester: Carcanet, 1996), pp. 213-15.

[3] Elizabeth Jennings, *Christianity and Poetry* (Fact and Faith Books 122) (London: Burns and Oates, 1965), pp. 11, 93. On poetic inspiration, see also H. D. [Hilda Doolittle], 'The Walls Do Not Fall: 20', in *Trilogy* (Manchester: Carcanet, 1973), p. 29.

[4] Jennings, *Christianity and Poetry*, p. 18.

[5] Jennings, *Christianity and Poetry*, p. 111.

[6] John F. A. Sawyer, *The Fifth Gospel: Isaiah in the History of Christianity* (Cambridge: Cambridge University Press, 1996), pp. 65-82, on 'The Cult of the Virgin Mary'.

[7] Whereas the Hebrew text of Isa 7.14 mentions a 'young woman' *('almah*), the Greek translation refers to a 'virgin' (*parthenos*).

[8] This wall painting, from the Roman Catacombs in the Church of St Priscilla, is noted by Sawyer, *The Fifth Gospel*, pp. 65, 76 (depicted in plate 3).

[9] For instance, much of the text of Handel's 1742 oratorio *Messiah* comes from the Book of Isaiah.

[10] For these themes, see also Isa. 45.8 and 1 Sam. 2. 1-8.

[11] See 'Agnus Dei' in Denise Levertov, *Selected Poems* (Newcastle upon Tyne: Bloodaxe Books, 1994), from 'Mass for the Day of St Thomas Didymus', pp. 175-181, especially p. 181: 'is not implied that *we* / must protect this perversely weak / animal, whose muzzle's nudgings / suppose there is milk to be found in us? Must hold to our icy hearts / a shivering God?'

[12] Gabriel's dealings with Joseph in W. H. Auden's *For the Time Being* have the heading 'The Temptation of St Joseph', with the result that Gabriel simply silences Joseph. See W. H. Auden, *Collected Longer Poems* (London: Faber and Faber, 1968), pp. 149-51. With grim realism, R. S. Thomas depicts Joseph teaching Jesus 'the true trade: to go / with the grain / he left me / For a new master / who put him to the fashioning / of a cross for himself'; see R. S. Thomas, 'Covenanters', in his *Collected Poems, 1945-1990* (London: Dent, 1993), pp. 404-406, at p. 405. See also George Mackay Brown, 'Stations of the Cross', in Archie Bevan and Brian Murray, eds, George Mackay Brown, *Collected Poems*, (London: Murray, 2005), pp. 178-92 ('Carpenter'), the carpenter on this occasion sends elsewhere the centurion who has come to order a gallows: 'Mary stood in the door, curling cold hands like leaves / Round the fruit of her womb. / "Hurray," she said, "let the saw sing. / Soon it will be time for the cradle to rock my boy"' (p. 184).

[13] On the woman named in Matthew's genealogy, see for example, Irene Nowell, 'Jesus' Great-Grandmothers: Matthew's Four and More', *Catholic Biblical Quarterly* 70 (2008): 1-15.

[14] Alice Miller, *Thou Shalt Not Be Aware: Society's Betrayal of the Child* (London: Pluto, 1991), p. 98.

[15] Miller, *Thou Shalt Not Be Aware*, p. 96.

[16] Pamela Vermes, *The Riddle of the Sparks* (Oxford: Foxcombe, 1993), p. 56; cf. Hos 1.10 (2.1).

[17] See, for instance, Elizabeth A. Johnson, *Truly Our Sister: A Theology of Mary in the Communion of Saints* (London: Continuum, 2003).

[18] A small photograph of the sculpture, completed in 2000, appears on Guy Reid's website (www.guyreidscuplture.com), which includes an excellent review of the work by Mark Vernon, 'Defrocking: Contested Images of Nudity in the Church', *New Statesman*, 5 February 2001. In addition, see 'The Virgin Punishing the Infant', after the 1926 painting by Max Ernst, in Carol Ann Duffy, *Selected Poems* (Harmondsworth: Penguin, 1994), p. 51. Ernst's painting initially had to be removed from the gallery in which it was first exhibited.

[19] Part of the poem 'Maria Sacerdota', by Alla Renee Bozarth, from Elizabeth Roberts and Elias Amidon, eds, *Life Prayers* (San Francisco, Cal.: Harper, 1996), p. 169, brought to my attention by the Rev'd Canon Dr Martin Warner of St Paul's Cathedral, London.

[20] Denise Levertov, *A Door in the Hive, with Evening Train* (Newcastle upon Tyne: Bloodaxe Books, 1993), p. 56.

[21] The Greek of Hab 3.2 adds the phrase (not found in the Hebrew text), 'You will be known in the midst of two living creatures'.

[22] Denise Levertov, 'The Nativity: An Altarpiece; A Door', *A Door in the Hive*, p. 92. For other poems in response to paintings, see R. S. Thomas, 'The Annunciation by Veneziano', in *Collected Poems*, p. 288, and the section 'Mary' from his poem 'Covenanters', in *Collected Poems*, pp. 404-405: David Scott, 'A Botticelli Nativity' (with a peacock getting itself settled on a stone wall before the kings arrive), in his *Selected Poems* (Newcastle upon Tyne: Bloodaxe Books, 1998), p. 137; William Carlos Williams, the fourth section, 'The Adoration of the Kings' of 'Pictures from Bruegel', in his *Collected Poems* Vol. 2, ed. Christopher MacGowan (London: Paladin, 1991), pp. 367-68.

[23] Les Murray, 'Animal Nativity', in *Collected Poems*, p. 389.

[24] U. A. Fanthorpe, 'The Sheepdog', in *Selected Poems* (London: Penguin, 1986), p. 117 . See also poems in George Mackay Brown, *The Wreck of the Archangel* (London: Murray, 1989): 'Midnight Words' (p. 102), with a child piping to welcome both kings and shepherds: 'Carol: Kings and Shepherds' (p. 103); 'Christmas Poem' (p. 104); and 'The Twelve Days of Christmas: Tinker Talk' (pp. 95- 96), which brings the Nativity within reach of Kirkwall on the Scottish island of Orkney.

[25] George Mackay Brown, 'Epiphany Poem', in *The Wreck of the Archangel*, p. 94. See also 'Desert Sleepers' (p. 54) and 'The Last Gate' (pp. 99- 100).

[26] George Mackay Brown, 'Desert Rose', in *The Wreck of the Archangel*, p. 97.

[27] George Mackay Brown, 'The Golden Door: The Three Kings', *Collected Poems*, pp. 149-150, at p. 150. See also 'Yule' (pp. 150-51); 'A Poem for Shelter' (p. 152); 'Stars: A Christmas Patchwork' (pp. 209-12).

[28] David Gascoyne, 'The Three Stars: A Prophecy', in *Selected Poems* (London: Enitharmon, 1994), pp. 102-103, at p. 103.

[29] Andrew Hudgkins, 'The Cestello Annunciation', in *Upholding Mystery: An Anthology of Contemporary Christian Poetry*, ed., David Impastato (New York: OUP, 1997), pp. 106-107, at p. 107, quoted by kind permission of Oxford University Press.

[30] Elizabeth Jennings, 'The Annunciation', in her *Collected Poems* (Manchester: Carcanet, 1986), pp. 45-6, at p. 46; see also 'Carol for 1997', in *Praises* (Manchester: Carcanet, 1998), p. 32. Compare Edwin Muir, 'The Annunciation', in his *Collected Poems* (London: Faber and Faber, 1979), pp. 223-24; and his lines about invoking God's Spirit to 'breathe and live', from his stanza of 'The Annunciation' in his *Selected Poems* (London: Faber and Faber, 1965), pp. 41-2.

[31] Denise Levertov, 'The Awoval', in *Oblique Prayers* (Newcastle upon Tyne: Bloodaxe Books, 1986), p. 70. See also the spirit within the natural world in her poem 'Passage' (p. 80).

[32] Levertov, *A Door in the Hive,* p. 87.

[33] Levertov, *A Door in the Hive*, pp. 87-88. And in 'Letter to a Friend' she wrote, 'Courage knows the price of living / Courage itself is a form of innocence, of trust or faith' (pp. 154-55, at p. 155). See also the memory of the 'intrepid girl' in Elizabeth Jennings' work, 'The Visitation', in *Collected Poems*, pp. 46-47.

[34] Tina Beattie, *God's Mother, Eve's Advocate: A Marian Narrative of Women's Salvation* (London: Continuum, 2000). Attend also to U2's song 'Grace', track 11 of *All That You Can't Leave Behind* (Universal International Music, 2000).

[35] R. S. Thomas, 'Mother and Child', in his *Collected Poems*, p. 461. See also William Carlos Williams, 'The Gift', in his *Collected Poems*, pp. 430-31, where the wise men whose gifts stood for all that love can bring see the child fed, and recognize it as a miracle, something

much more valuable-gold become milk. In Elizabeth Jennings' 'Meditation on the Nativity' (*Collected Poems*, p. 116), 'her modesties divest / Our guilt of shame as she hands him her food / And he smiles on her breast'.

[36] Elizabeth Jennings, '1 The Fear', from 'Christmas Suite in Five Movements', in her *Collected Poems*, pp. 178-81, at p. 178.

[37] Judith Wright, 'Night and the Child' , in her *Collected Poems 1942-1985* (Manchester: Carcanet, 1994), pp. 61-62, at p. 61. See also her poem 'The World and the Child' (pp. 36-37).

[38] On Simeon, see Denise Levertov, *Breathing the Water* (Newcastle upon Tyne : Bloodaxe Books, 1998), p. 65; for a brief reflection on Candlemas, see part of Amy Clampitt, 'A Procession at Candlemas', in Fleur Adcock, ed., *The Faber Book of 20th Century Women's Poetry* (London: Faber and Faber, 1987), pp. 153-58, at p. 154, where she speaks of the Virgin Mary carrying 'fire as though it were a flower', on the supposition that God 'might actually need a mother'. Denise Levertov's political activism after her move to the United States took many forms, one of which was her poem 'Advent 1966' (*Selected Poems*, p. 84), in which Robert Southwell's 'Burning Babe' as an image of redemption is transposed to an image of horror in the burning bodies of children in Vietnam.

[39] Carol Ann Duffy, *The World's Wife* (London: Picador, 1999), pp. 7-10.

[40] H. D., *Trilogy*, pp. 113-72, at p. 172

[41] H. D., *Trilogy*, p. 123.

[42] David Gascoyne, 'Birch of a Prince', from his *Collected Poems* (Oxford: Oxford University Press, 1965), p. 170, quoted by kind permission of Oxford University Press.

6

Mary: For Now

In this chapter I am as it were beginning again, that is to say, I am not in any sense reviewing what I have written in the past but am attempting to ascertain and evaluate what has been or may be made of 'Mary' in our time and in many different places. I agree with Ursula King that notwithstanding the ambivalence present in many or most of our attempts to make sense of our experiences, the Christian tradition in all its social and historical complexity may still offer 'a horizon of hope' for those who engage with it, marked as it may be with thanksgiving and celebration both within and beyond Christian institutions.[1] So on the one hand we must necessarily address some of the disastrous consequences for women, and therefore also for men of some forms of Christianity, but also attend to fresh sources of insight and aspiration from wherever these arise, however cautiously we attend to what may be on offer, and whatever the consequences of giving them attention.[2] For what is required is a theological project that will intersect 'the borders and boundaries of class, caste, gender, ethnicity, nationality, religion and ability' to be true to lived experience, believing that God takes the side of the 'unbelongers' who bring about change.[3] Surprises may well be in store as we attempt to reconstrue 'incarnational' faith, not only in the work of those who have appropriated the insights of, for example, Luce Irigaray[4] and Julia Kristeva,[5] but in the insights of those who draw on the Christian tradition while they continue to inhabit and represent it in a host of different ways. My first two examples draw attention to two authors both of whom established themselves in the days when institutional positions to teach theology were not available to lay women in the Church of England, but both of whom made their own distinctive contributions to appreciate the possible significance of Marian traditions and devotions in their time: the first half of the twentieth century. Both provoke questions and concerns of present-day importance, arguably intrinsic to any serious consideration of Mary.

Evelyn Underhill

Evelyn Underhill (born in 1875) sought to establish herself as both poet and novelist before becoming known first within the Church of England as of central importance in the rediscovery of 'mysticism' (more commonly identified at the present time as 'spirituality') and the importance of a life of prayer, pioneering and establishing a retreat movement for both men and women, lecturing and writing theology, with an extensive list of publications to her credit. She became the first woman Fellow of King's College, London, and was offered the degree of Doctor of Divinity by the University of Aberdeen in 1938, though unfortunately was too ill with asthma and bronchitis to undertake the long journey from London (she died in 1941).[6] Our focus at this point is on the importance to her of what she discovered on holidays in mainland Europe before the devastation of World War I, recorded in notebook entries between 1901-1907.[7] In Vincenza, Italy, she found written the Mysteries of the Rosary in the arcade which stretched from the plain to the church of the Madonna del Monte; in the Cathedral of Carcassonne, France, a Pieta: Our Lady, 'full of sense and full of sadness, who has retained a vulnerable heart. Her child at this moment is helpless, quiet and at peace as she supports his head, as in His babyhood. She suffers but is content to suffer, knowing it now well with Him, at the cost of loneliness for her', in quiet, steadfast, grieving affection.[8] This appreciation then appears in Underhill's second novel, in which Mary actually addresses Catherine, one of the central characters in the novel. When on her honeymoon visit to Carcassonne, Catherine believes that she will have to abandon her husband, fearing that she has ruined his creativity. For Mary's long days of love and pain, her son going to sacrifice whilst she 'would have suffered hell so willingly to save Him' enable her so to console Catherine that she is able to remain with her husband no matter what that may demand from her in love and pain.[9] We owe to Carol Poston attention both to Evelyn Underhill's 1906 translation and selection of *The Miracles of Our Lady*[10] but also her meditations on the Rosary, *The Spiral Way*, published perhaps wisely under the assumed (masculine) name of John Cordelier which came out in 1912, that is just the year after the publication of her first major book on mysticism.[11] She would not have wanted to jeopardise the importance of what she wanted to commend by raising 'Protestant' hackles by attending to a form of devotion so unfamiliar to many of her contemporaries. In one important respect, however, she rightly drew on the text which recorded Mary's presence at Pentecost (Acts 1:14) having seen early representations of the scene, Mary as Spirit-Bearer, 'flaming charity'.[12] However, she never lost sight of the importance of Mary (as Blessed Virgin) as she made clear in her second major book at the conclusion of a long career of teaching and writing. For in her *Worship* published in 1936, she warmly commended attention to the saints of Catholic worship both western and eastern, and especially to Mary 'as the human agent of the Incarnation', one of those who enabled 'the divine charity and beauty tabernacle among men.' And in the same paragraph she made the most important point which applies not only to reflection on Mary, but more widely in respect of religious devotion—whatever the apparent 'phantasies, superstitions, and sentimentalisms' we may discern in a particular religious tradition, we should not allow ourselves to be blinded 'to the deep spiritual truth' which it may enshrine.[13] The particular truth for her in her time and place, in the appalling social and political circumstances of Europe after the first World War, required the teaching and practice of intercessory prayer, including prayer for enemies, and the sacrificial life she discerned in Mary (enduring pain and suffering which she cannot prevent). For her own part, Evelyn Underhill came to express this in pacifism.[14] What form of political activism, including intercessory prayer and pacifism, may be required in other circumstances is a question Underhill arguably leaves with us from her understanding and appropriation of Mary.[15]

Dorothy L. Sayers

Towards the end of this chapter we will turn to 'trauma' theology for another mode of response to acute distress and its consequences. For the moment, however, we turn to another woman theologian of the first part of the twentieth century, not a pacifist, but in a different way preoccupied with Mary: Dorothy L. Sayers.[16] Like Evelyn Underhill, Sayers was a beneficiary of the social, economic and educational changes of the late nineteenth and early twentieth centuries and enjoyed an excellent education especially in languages. Almost twenty years younger than Underhill, Dorothy L. Sayers came to maturity during the First World War and lived through the political and economic turmoil in Europe and beyond which led to the Second World War, attempting for her part to argue for social reconstruction as and when the war came to an end.[17] She was therefore

of the generation which both had to face up to the industrialised slaughter
of twentieth-century battlefields, as well as to the evidence of organised
slaughter of civilian populations whether in extermination camps or those
which 'concentrated' hosts of people to be worked to death, or slaughtered
by means of nuclear or 'conventional' aerial bombing campaigns. Whereas
Evelyn Underhill was daughter of one successful lawyer, married another
lawyer, and remained childless, and so pioneered an extraordinary mode
of life for herself without having to earn her own living, Dorothy Sayers'
circumstances reflected a somewhat different world. Her excellent education
begun in a clerical household made possible graduation from Oxford in
1920. Like Evelyn Underhill she found publishers for some poetry,[18] but
circumstances which included her love affair which left her with a son
to support (the boy was raised in a friend's household where she visited
him as his 'adoptive' mother), and her marriage to a divorced man whose
children remained with their mother made it imperative that she find work
in which she could make enough money to live on. So she produced an
explicitly combative stance on the value and importance of women in both
church and society[19]—matters hardly resolved to this day, depending on the
interplay of religious tradition and social and political circumstance.

Success as a translator (again in common with Evelyn Underhill) was
outstripped by her success both as novelist and playwright, and whereas
Underhill's pilgrim in Vincenza as it were expressed devotion to Mary by
saying the Rosary when climbing up to the church there, Dorothy L. Sayers
took advantage of the new medium of broadcasting to portray Mary in a
different mode of 'performance', and beyond that, most seriously in a play
written for Lichfield Cathedral.[20] In her introduction to the published version
of the first play, *He that Should Come,* written for broadcasting on Christmas
Day 1938, she made clear her intention in setting it in the courtyard of a
busy inn, so as to show 'the miracle that was to change the whole course of
human life enacted in a world casual, inattentive, contemptuous, absorbed
in its own affairs and completely unaware of what was happening'.[21] It
is Balthazar from Ethiopia (one of the kings of the developed traditions
derived from the first Gospel of the Christian Scriptures) who expresses
the profound hope in a time of fear, seeking God beside him, 'bearing the
weight of his own creation', his 'voice among the voices of the vanquished,'
his 'hand touching Balthazar's in the darkness, a face upon which he can
look, eyes in which can be read that "He is acquainted with grief."'[22] For
once, Joseph is given a major role, not least in repeating the words of the
angel of the Annunciation to Mary, who herself speaks to the shepherds of

her son's forthcoming kingdom.[23] It is she, at the centre of the Holy Family, who shows to the kings 'the wisdom of the innocent', 'the power of the helpless', and to Balthazar, 'God made man'.[24]

In a complete cycle of plays (*The Man Born to be King*) written for radio and delivered between December 1941 and October 1942, the first play, 'Kings in Judea,' in three scenes extended her reflections on the Nativity.[25] This time she wrote her own notes on the characters, so that Balthazar, for instance, has 'the temperament of the mystic, and his interest is in the relationship of man to men and of men to God. His wisdom is the wisdom of the heart.'[26] And it is he who believes that it would be possible to bear fear and suffering if God shared the miseries of his own world. 'For the riddle that torments the world is this: Shall Sorrow and Love be reconciled at last, when the promised Kingdom comes?' To him Mary herself interprets the words of the angelic annunciation, knowing that 'Wisdom and Power and Sorrow *can* live together with Love' the child in her arms being the answer to all the riddles.[27] This first cycle concludes with Joseph fleeing with Mary and the child down to Egypt, to avoid massacre, which may include many who have no choice about why they die. Remembrance of Mary and of 'Holy Innocents' might well continue to alert us to 'the ongoing and expanding catalogue of evils and agonies that connect the suffering of the past to those of the present.'[28] And the flight of the family to Egypt also prompts a 'migrant reading', with 'men who work toward the saving of this child— the magi and Joseph.' It is the person of Joseph who 'paves the way for a different or new understanding of masculinity... for he gives up his own power for a positive and transformative masculinity'. He thus may remind us of 'the many fathers who risk their lives for the sake of their children and die trying to protect them by taking them and their children on hazardous journeys in search of life and a future'. They denounce terror by fleeing, and their flight is 'both an act of courage as much as it is a quest for life.'[29] In addition, the tears of Rachel (Jer. 31:13-15) and the daughter Zion of *Lamentations* praying for divine compassion emerge in many a context, not least in the twentieth and twenty-first centuries.[30]

In the third play, *A Certain Nobleman*, Dorothy L. Sayers follows the fourth Gospel in juxtaposing the miracle at Cana with the temple-cleansing incident, so as to show 'the human mother faced with the reality of what her Son's personality and vocation mean in practice', her first encounter with his divine power, being 'saddened and gladdened by it.'[31] In the eleventh play, 'King of Sorrows', Mary's character is indicated as having 'that stillness and prenatural lucidity which sometimes accompany extreme anguish of mind'. Mary has two long speeches in the first scene: one expressing 'a sort of settled acceptance of the intolerable', the second with 'the clairvoyance of prophecy'.[32] To begin with, she recollects her care for a son as a child, now facing that there is nothing she can do. 'This is the worst thing; to conceive beauty in your heart and bring it forth into the world, and then to stand by helpless and watch it suffer'; but then, 'I know now what he is, and what I am … I, Mary, am the fact; God is the truth; but Jesus is fact and truth—he is reality. You cannot see the immortal truth till it is born in the flesh of the fact… the feet that must walk this road were made of me'.[33] And finally, in 'the suggestion of a Pieta, she asks for her son to be given into her arms', recognising the presence of Balthazar who had given the gift of myrrh, and awaiting the gift of frankincense.[34]

Quite unexpectedly, Mary as it were makes one final appearance in Dorothy L. Sayers' drama, in the play commissioned by the Chapter (the Governing Body) of Lichfield Cathedral, which already in 1943 was planning for a service of Thanksgiving for the preservation of the Cathedral, together with a Pageant to celebrate seven hundred and fifty years since its foundation, which was due to fall in 1945.[35] First performed in 1946, it was broadcast in 1947. The matter to which Sayers determined to address herself was the inextricable commitment to injustice in the course of a war fought in part to re-establish justice—that injustice being the deliberate and systematic bombing of cites one after another, no matter what the cost to their civilian populations. The policy both then and now remains controversial, so much so that it took until 2012 for a memorial to the crews of Bomber Command to be erected in London.[36] In her play, Dorothy L. Sayers imagines one of the shot-down airmen in the moment of his death, drawn back into the fraternity of his natal city, indeed beyond the 'bloody alternatives' of bombing a city or not bombing a concentration camp, either way condemning thousands to death, but now joining his 'fellow victims/And fellow criminals in the exchange of blood'.[37] The play includes the Chorus pleading for 'Mary of pity' to speak, choose for the city, and Gabriel sent to Mary. The Chorus asks, 'What will the city do now, if a girl refuse/The weight of glory, the seven swords in the heart?' The scene of the Annunciation concludes with the 'Persona Dei' saying 'Woman, behold thy Son', and Mary's response, 'Behold Thy Mother' (from the scene in the fourth Gospel where uniquely among the Gospels the writer places Mary 'near the crucified': see John 19:26-27).

It is at this point that Dorothy L. Sayers makes explicit her major source of inspiration for the title of her play and for the role Mary plays

within it. Circumstances combined had turned her back not merely to a
re-reading of Dante's *Divine Comedy* but to its translation, accompanied
by her own admirable introductory notes and comments on the text, not
merely explaining how Dante's text related to the circumstances of his day,
but to her own, and its forms of embodied damnation and corruption.[38] A
key phrase from the third volume, *Paradise* is 'the just vengeance,' which is
found in Dante's reflection on the Incarnation and divine self-giving, and it
is redemption and the celebration of resurrection which is explored in her
play for Lichfield.[39] What Dorothy L. Sayers introduced at this point were
the first six lines of Canto 33 of *Paradise*, sung as a hymn by a choir.[40] These
words came from St Bernard's prayer to the Virgin, which she had used on
her Christmas cards,[41] prayer to the 'Virgin Mother, daughter of thy Son ...'.
She is given a speech comparable to those of an earlier play (from her Son's
birth and childhood up to his final journey into Jerusalem) and on the way
to Calvary, invites men 'made in the image of God' to see the burden laid on
one Man's shoulder: 'For the flesh faints and falls with the heavy weight of
the glory/But the power of the Godhead is enough for all mankind.' Thus,
she herself becomes the interpreter of her Son's actions, and the pilot stands
with her at the foot of the cross, themselves receiving the exchange of son
and mother from the crucified one. As he dies, commending himself to
God, so too the pilot trusts himself into God's hands and he greets her as 'O
Mary of the seven swords of sorrow ...'. There remains one extraordinary
moment for Mary, who at this very point recalls how the 'very Lord of glory'
lay wrapped in swathing bands, as the Chorus takes over, who now will be
wrapped in grave-bands, funeral spices mixed with myrrh. She is given one
last, brief speech in praise of the City of resurrection life,[42] with its great
'company of the robes of light'.

The Cathedral setting and the doctrinal framework shaping the play via
the writings of Dante, were profoundly different from the Nativity play *He
That Should Come*, set in the courtyard, though both are faithful in different
ways to the interplay of biblical text, doctrine and tradition characteristic
of reflection on Mary. Furthermore, both the work of Evelyn Underhill and
of Dorothy L. Sayers inadvertently make clear the integral connection that
needs explicitly to be made between what is said about Mary and what is
said about the Holy Spirit and 'divine immanence'.[43] At the present time, this
is exemplified by Sir James Macmillan, who in both his compositions and
his own reflections on his work suggests that Mary's receptivity to the Holy
Spirit in the Annunciation provides the model for his own understanding
and suggests 'arts' broadly conceived.[44] Both Macmillan's 'Quickening' (on

reverence for life) in collaboration with poet Michael Symmons Roberts, and MacMillan's Choral Symphony No.5, with its alternative title, 'Le Grand Inconnu—The Mystery of the Holy Spirit', were central to performances in the 2019 Edinburgh Festival.[45] It is beyond the compass of this chapter to attend in detail to much of the development of the interplay between 'theology and the arts', to which Dorothy L. Sayers deliberately gave such stimulus in her day, though we may at least acknowledge some publications in different forms.[46]

Dorothy L. Sayers died before the Second Vatican Council (1962-1965) and the extraordinary impact that Council had both within and beyond the Roman Catholic Church, not least because on the one hand the documents of the Council included a chapter on 'The Blessed Virgin Mary, Mother of God, in the Mystery of Christ and the Church', whilst on the other, Pope Paul VI proclaimed her 'Mother of the Church'.[47] This chapter will attend to the central importance of 'Mother of God' in the traditions of the Orthodox Churches (again, pioneered by Evelyn Underhill),[48] but first stress the wholly unpredictable impact of developments of reflection on Mary as women gained access to theological education, in the course of which new forms of spirituality, commentary and evaluation of 'Mary' were to emerge.[49] In respect of Mary it becomes clear that the power of a tradition lies in its ability 'to respond to changing needs and experience rather than in any requirement for uniformity or a single line of development.'[50] Of central importance was the way the Council affirmed that God had always remained faithful to his covenant with Israel. One significant development in what became feminist theology has been the entirely appropriate determination to enlighten the subject of 'Mary' (among many other topics) via the firm correction of misapprehension about Jewish tradition, vital as is its importance for understanding Christian texts, traditions and doctrines, with in addition specifically Jewish commentary on the texts of the Gospels, since these lie at the heart of any concern with Mary.[51] There remains one outstanding contribution to understanding Mary both for locating her in Jewish tradition, and for ecumenical understanding, before attending to the new appearance of Mary in 'trauma theology' which brings Mary into a renewal of theology for now.

Margaret Barker, re-reading the Bible, and learning from Orthodoxy

In turning to Margaret Barker (another 'independent scholar' akin to the two examples of women 'forebears' in theology with which this chapter began, albeit in Barker's case a Methodist, and a former President of the

Society for Old Testament Studies), two features of her work are especially noteworthy. One is her wholly original appreciation of the possible roots of tradition about Mary which may be found in Christian Scripture; the other is that she has made possible the appreciation of the doctrine and traditions of the Orthodox churches, without which efforts towards 'ecumenism' proceed up a blind alley. With massive learning (including all the relevant 'ancient' languages) she has been central to restoring the significance of the Temple in Jerusalem for the origins of Christianity. A crucial moment for her came one February when present at an episcopal liturgy of the Orthodox Church, when she realised that she was looking at 'temple ritual'. One of her most controversial discussions has to do with her contention that the first Temple had been the residence of 'the Great Lady', who can be discerned initially in the book of Isaiah, a text with a complex history,[52] and beyond, both in Hebrew and Greek-speaking Jewish culture.[53] From its earliest days, Christian tradition was concerned with the restoration of the 'Lady' to places of worship and the ikons which portrayed her with her traditional symbols. Appreciation of this tradition makes possible a re-reading of the Gospels, as does taking seriously the phenomenon of 'theophany', not least in respect of prophetic experience of God and the 'Son' of the 'Lady', and appropriation of the significance of the 'woman clothed with the sun' for Mary as a powerful figure of divine transformation, a theme we may appreciate in Orthodox theology.[54]

It is now possible to value the remarkable sixth-century poetry of Romanos 'the Melodist' in its 'poetic configuration' of biblical themes and hagiography, bearing in mind that it may have been sung both at the end of a liturgy and even outside church walls, drawing in the listeners with refrains for them to sing.[55] Re-writing the scene of 'annunciation' Romanos has Gabriel ask himself 'how can the exalted join the lowly in love?' He then gives Mary her own voice in exploring her own feelings to herself, her first response being to think, 'What am I seeing? What shall I ask?', and finding her courage as she shakes Gabriel into referring to the scripture portion of Moses drying up the sea which flowed again. To this she replies, 'If you were not from above, you wouldn't have explained the words of Scripture, / but being from light, you straitened whatever was tangled.' Gabriel's departure enables Mary to summon Joseph who to begin with is paralyzed by what he sees: 'burning heat and snowstorm, a paradise and a furnace, / a smoking mountain, a divine flower sprouting, / an awesome throne, a lowly footstool/ of the All-Merciful One /...' Unfortunately the text ends with Joseph's determination to send her away: 'For me it is clear that the light of your virginity shines, yet for those in the dark, it is quenched, as they are unworthy of knowing you'.[56]

The 'scene' of the annunciation apart, merely referring to 'Theotokos'— Mother of the Lord—without further attention misses her significance as a sovereign patron and defender of Constantinople, one who rules the world and prevails over all, herself preaching salvation to living and dead alike.[57] Sensitive alignment of early Christian literature and liturgy is thus extended and developed by Orthodox theologians, but given special attention in the work of Margaret Barker, the one person capable of bringing to bear her own understanding of the portrayal of Mary as Holy Wisdom, both of vital importance for the history of Jerusalem and its temple, which she established over a quarter of a century ago.[58] To take one brief selection of what she found in just a sample of liturgical texts she finds that Jewish tradition remembered things which were associated with lady wisdom and which appear as titles of Mary: the menorah, the ark, the Spirit, the Fire, the cherubim, the anointing oil, manna and the high priestly staff, and there are many more.[59] Sheer incomprehension both of this imagery and its poetic expression in liturgy are unfortunately perplexing in contemporary culture, whether given music such as John Tavener's composition for cello and strings following the pattern of the Feasts of Mary, *The Protecting Veil* (from an appearance of Mary in a church in Constantinople—her manifestation of powerful protection), or David Bintley's ballet to that music. The 'veil' begins as Mary's shawl, becomes the wrappings for the infant Christ, the Veronica cloth, and Christ's burial shroud—discarded at his resurrection.[60]

Karen O'Donnell and trauma theology

Finally, given that I began this chapter with reference to the Pieta and the 'Stabat Mater', images we reflect on the significance of Mary in respect of the new area of theology, 'trauma theology', given voice in work addressed to veterans of armed conflict and those who mourn for them, whether 'Mary' or 'Rachel'.[61] It is Karen O'Donnell who foregrounds the 'Annunciation-Incarnation' event in re-membering her own experiences, all too familiar in the lives of women.[62] Whilst there is no single definition of trauma, many forms of violence and abuse are well within the range of 'ordinary experience', but it may usefully be understood as the experience of 'rupture' in bodily integrity, together with someone's 'memory timeline', which may involve both flashbacks and nightmares. There is also the possibility of rupture in 'cognition and language' that is, someone may be unable to remember or access the trauma in such a way as to be able to understand it, or if remembered, to have no language to give an account of what happened, and their past or present feelings about it. Above all, 'bodies and remembering lie at the heart of trauma and trauma recovery', once someone has established that they are indeed safe, able to remember and narrate what happened, helped by witnesses who will hear and support that narrative.[63] O'Donnell's prime example of trauma is her personal experience of 'repeated reproductive loss', the sense of loss of an recoverable young self, and acute distress at the inappropriate 'theology' offered her and other 'miscarrying' women.[64] The fundamental contention of O'Donnell's book is that learning to love one's re-membered body is learning to love the bodies of the Annunciation-Incarnation event. Whilst the conviction that 'God suffers' has long been contentious, Karen O'Donnell follows both Luther and Moltmann on the significance of Christ's Passion within the Trinity, in that she suggests a miscarrying woman may reveal 'what it means to hold a place of death within oneself, even as one lives'[65] which may be an image of comfort: 'God with us'.

Since it is Mary who 'first offers up the bodily elements that will become the flesh and blood of Christ' and who makes her agreement with the work of God, she provides the role model for a priest, participating 'with the Spirit' in the particular revelation of Christ, the divine already present in all things, the source of nourishment and life.[66] Running through the whole book are many constructive proposals about what follows from renewed perception of both tradition and doctrine, but especially important are the pages which vividly consider the Annunciation-Incarnation event as trauma, for 'Mary must have been shocked and overwhelmed' by her experience of 'angelic visitation and a subsequent miraculous pregnancy', for her bodily integrity is ruptured by the sudden presence, of another life, inside her. The enfleshment of the divine Son in her womb is a physical rupturing of her flesh to make way for the flesh of another, 'a dramatic disturbance in the temporal order'. She experiences a failure to say what has happened to her, but her recovery begins with finding a place of safety with her relative, Elizabeth. She is transformed into a new person, voiced in Luke 1:46-55, finding herself to be blessed by God the Mighty One, returning home with her pregnancy established, and proclaiming both divine mercy and divine justice.[67]

For Karen O'Donnell, learning to love Mary's body meant 'not relegating her to a walk-on part in the nativity or the role of silent, weeping mother at the Cross'. Rather it meant learning to love her 'in the fullness of her embodied experience', and the bodies all women, as women in the fullness of their embodied experiences, all 'made possible by and as a response to the love of God.'[68] Although her work is that of someone wholly committed to traditional Marian doctrines of the Roman Catholic Church[69]—some of which are shared neither with Orthodox Christians let with other ecclesial congregations - hers is surely exemplary in re-reading and imaging Mary in the light of changing circumstances, experience and understanding. Love and a response to love may take many forms not least in regarding Mary as the embodiment both not merely of hope but of the courage by which it may be recognised. As we have seen in some of the examples I have cited above, hope may take the form of pacifism, of enduring conflict in the determination to bring horrors to an end, of single-minded determination to remedy distress and evil, of sustained attention to traumas of different kinds, including the betrayal of sympathy and support. We may even add the need for a Marian sensitivity for pitching into politics at all levels to bring about change for the better, for instance to eliminate intolerable conditions in which people may live and work, or live and die homeless and half-starved. We may not have discerned in Mary the inspiration to attend to new circumstances, but arguably need to do so to make sense of Mary—for now.

NOTES TO CHAPTER 6

¹ Ursula King, 'Women and Christianity—A Horizon of Hope', in Teresa Elwes ed., *Women's Voices. Essays in Contemporary Feminist Theology* (London: Marshall Pickering, 1992), pp.147-158. See also Grace Jantzen on 'a theological aesthetics' which looks to 'the splendour within the world', fashioned by beauty, welcoming 'multiple shapes and curves and differences', addressing the question, 'what do you long for most of all, and what are you doing to prevent it?' in Janet Martin Soskice and Diana Lipton, eds, *Feminism and Theology* (Oxford: Oxford University Press, 2003), pp. 344-355, at p.354. An introduction to issues of 'gender' and its expression in society and culture, including the acquisition of language, embodied and sexual experience, social relationships, the pursuit and application of knowledge, may be found in Elaine Graham, *Making the Difference: Gender, Personhood and Theology* (London: Mowbray, 1995).

² An unavoidable example of the deplorable consequence of setting 'Mary' over against other women is to be found in the work of Marcella Althaus-Reid, 'When God is a rich white woman who does not walk: the hermeneutical circle of Mariology in Latin America', in *From Feminist Theology to Indecent Theology* (London: SCM Press, 2004), 30-43, on submission in either wealth or poverty, and the need to find 'a *Maria* among us' maybe a street vendor, a child in the slums, a battered woman, or a *chica* cleaning the home of the rich lady, or a woman who is not white or rich and is longing to walk, p.43. See also Marcella Althaus-Reid, 'Doing a Theology from Disappeared Bodies: Theology, Sexuality, and the Excluded Bodies of the Discourses of Latin American Liberation Theology', in Mary McClinton Fulkerson and Sheila Briggs eds., *The Oxford Handbook of Feminist Theology* (Oxford: Oxford University Press, 2012), pp. 441-455. Another example is Eve Rebecca Parker, 'The Virgin and the Whore—An Interreligious Challenge for Our Times: Exploring the Politics of Religious Belonging with Tamar', *The Ecumenical Review* 71 (2019): 693-705.

³ Parker, 'The Virgin and the Whore', p. 705.

⁴ For example, Rasa Luzyte, *A Thealogy of Mary: the non-Christian View of Mary, the Shadow of Mary and an individual Connection to the Divine Self through Mary and an individual connection to the Divine Self through Mary*, PhD thesis, University of Stirling, 2013, argues for a non-Christian framework, perceived as 'a sacred place for self-analysis, reflection and the recovery of instincts' (p. 221). She finds a divine, powerful, sovereign and charismatic Mary to be found in Lithuanian legends, courageous enough to turn back the enemy, faithful to herself, 'at home' in 'the very women whose souls Mary is mending' (p. 204). In them Mary in turn finds her own home, builds her own church and finds her own followers. In a more 'orthodox' mode, using examples from Latin America and Karelia see Elina Vuola, '*La Morenita* on Skis; Women's Popular Marian Piety and Feminist Research on Religion', in Mary McClinton Fulkerson and Sheila Briggs eds, *The Oxford Handbook of Feminist Theology* (Oxford: Oxford University Press, 2012), pp. 494-524, drawing both on anthropology and folklore, on Mary as exemplary human being and exemplary woman as well, understanding the pains and contradictions of life. As maternal friend and divine figure she symbolises both the possibility of 'female deification' and herself represents and expresses the deeply human aspect of the divine (pp. 516-518).

⁵ Alison Jasper, 'Feminism, Religion and this Incredible Need to Believe: working with Julia Kristeva Again', *Feminist Theology* 21 (2013): 279-294. The author commends what she has perceived in Kristeva's work – always to question, to submit assumptions about what is fundamental and trustworthy to interrogation, 'but above all, to believe that we can do this' (p.293).

⁶ See Ann Loades, 'Mysticism: "The Energetic Love" of a Female Adventurer', in Louise Nelstrop and Simon D. Podmore, eds., *Exploring Lost Dimensions in Christian Mysticism: Opening to the Mystical* (Farnham: Ashgate, 2013), pp. 117-129. The first doctorates for theological studies conferred upon women by universities in Europe were awarded variously to Margaret Gibson and Agnes Lewis by the universities of Halle, Heidelberg, Trinity

College Dublin and in 1904 the University of St Andrews. See Rebecca J.W. Jefferson, 'A fresh appreciation of the Scholarship of Agnes Smith Lewis and Margaret Dunlop Gibson', *Medieval Feminist Forum: Journal for the Society for Medieval Feminist Scholarship* 45 (2009): 23-49. The publication of their discoveries included Agnes' 'Select Narratives of Holy Women'. Oxford did not admit women to the degrees of BA/MA until 1920; Cambridge in 1948.

[7] Evelyn Underhill (ed. Lucy Menzies), *Shrines and Cities of France and Italy* (London: Longmans, Green and Co., 1949). Lucy Menzies became a partner in Evelyn Underhill's work in many ways, and herself became the first woman to be awarded a DD degree in 1954 by the University of St Andrews, her hometown.

[8] Underhill, *Shrines and Cities*, pp.65, 87.

[9] Evelyn Underhill, *The Lost Word* (London: Heinemann,1907), pp. 294-295. For discussion of all three of her novels, see Ann Loades, 'Evelyn Underhill (1875-1941): Mysticism in Fiction', in Judith Maltby and Alison Shell eds., *Anglican Women Novelists* (London: T & T Clark, 2019), pp. 72-84, with extensive bibliography on Underhill's work at pp. 227-233, and adding Robyn Wrigley-Carr, *The Spiritual Development of Evelyn Underhill* (London: SPCK 2020).

[10] Evelyn Underhill, *The Miracles of Our Lady Saint Mary Brought out of Divers Tongues and Newly Set Forth in English* (New York, N.Y.: E. P. Dutton, 1906).

[11] Carol H. Poston, 'Evelyn Underhill and the Virgin Mary', *Anglican Theological Review* 97 (2015): 75-89. We may also bear in mind the probably support and influence of a cousin, Francis Underhill, like her an Anglo-Catholic 'Modernist' with a faith robust enough to take on the challenges of a post war world, who became Bishop of Bath and Wells; and also the indubitable evidence of the 'social theology' of that particular ecclesial culture. Social activism was not directly Evelyn Underhill's vocation, as for instance was the case for Mary Lily Walker (1863-1913) (on whom, see Eddie Small, *Forgotten Visionary of Dundee* [Dundee: Dundee University Press, 2013]), much though she relished the 'practical' gifts of many of the 'mystics' she studied. For insight into appalling conditions in the first half of the twentieth century, see for example, Jennifer Worth, *Shadows of the Workhouse* (London: Weidenfeld and Nicolson, 2005).

[12] Poston, 'Evelyn Underhill and the Virgin Mary', p. 87. On Mary and Acts 1.13-15, and a 'Biblical Mission Mandate' for Africa and its troubles, see Musimbi Kanyoro, 'Thinking Mission in Africa', in Amy-Jill Levine with Marianne Blickenstaff, eds, *A Feminist Companion to the Acts of the Apostles* (London: T & T Clark International, 2004), pp. 61-70; Albert C. Labriola 'The Bible and Iconography', in Michael Lieb, Emma Mason and Jonathan Roberts, eds, *The Oxford Handbook of the Reception History of the Bible* (Oxford: OUP, 2011), pp. 175-199, especially pp.197-198.

[13] Evelyn Underhill, *Worship* (Guildford: Eagle, 1991), pp 192-193. She remains rare among theologians in writing about worship/adoration, both in this book and in shorter presentations to different groups.

[14] See further Ann Loades, 'Evelyn Underhill (1875-1941): Mysticism and Worship', *International Journal for the Study of the Christian Church* 10 (2010): 57-70.

[15] See Christine Chinkin, 'Ending impunity and prioritising survivors', *British Academy Review* 36 (2019): 11-14, on international attempts to counter 'the perpetation of sexual violence in armed conflict'.

[16] On Dorothy L. Sayers as a novelist, see Jessica Martin, 'Dorothy L. Sayers (1893-1957): God and the Detective', in Judith Maltby and Alison Shell, eds, *Anglican Women Novelists* (London: T & T Clark, 2018), pp. 87-101. On her development of Peter Wimsey as a character, and his commitment to the principled pursuit of truth and justice, see Ann Loades, 'Dorothy L. Sayers: War and Redemption', in David Hein and Edward Henderson, eds., *C.S. Lewis and Friends: Faith and the Power of Imagination* (London: SPCK, 2011), pp. 53-70.

[17] See part 7, 'London Calling' for a selection of her writing on hope for the future in Ann Loades, ed., *Dorothy L. Sayers: Spiritual Writings* (London: SPCK, 1993), pp. 120-143, a book which offers an introduction to the scope of her work, by means of extracts from her writings. A comprehensive re-evaluation of her achievements will appear in Frances Clemson, *Showing Forth God's Act in History: Theology and Drama in the Work of Dorothy L. Sayers* (London: T & T Clark, 2022).

[18] Neither of them produced work comparable to that of Christina Rossetti, for instance: see Rachel Mann, *In the Bleak Midwinter. Through Advent and Christmas with Christina Rossetti* (Norwich: Canterbury Press, 2019).

[19] Compare Evelyn Underhill, 'The Ideals of the Ministry of Women' (1932), *Mixed Pasture* (London: Methuen 1933), pp.113-122, and Dorothy L. Sayers' essays of 1938/1941 published in her *Unpopular Opinions* (London: Gollancz, 1946), discussed in 'The Sacramentalist's Agenda,' part 3 of Ann Loades, *Feminist Theology. Voices from the Past* (Oxford: Polity/Blackwell, 2001), pp. 167-192.

[20] Many of her plays are now republished in paperback by Wipf and Stock, Eugene, Oregon, 2011.

[21] Dorothy L. Sayers, *He that Should Come: A Nativity Pay in One Act,* 'Note to Producers', p.29.

[22] Sayers, *He That Should Come*, p.39.

[23] Sayers, *He That Should Come*, p. 83, p. 99. On one of the rare representations of Joseph, see 'The Role of Joseph', in Sarah Drummond, *Divine Conception: The Art of the Annunciation* (London: Unicorn, 2018), pp. 40-51.

[24] Sayers, *He That Should Come*, p.100.

[25] Dorothy L. Sayers, *The Man Born to be King: A Play-Cycle on the Life of our Lord and Saviour Jesus Christ* (London: Gollancz, 1947), pp. 43-66

[26] Sayers, *The Man Born to be King* p.44.

[27] Sayers, *The Man Born to be King* pp.58-59.

[28] Bridget Nichols, 'The Feast of the Holy Innocents and Anglican Remembering', *Anaphora* 13 (2019): pp. 1-28.

[29] Monica Jyotsna Melancthon, 'The Flight to Egypt: a Migrant Reading – Implications for a Lutheran Understanding of Salvation', in Kenneth Mtata and Craig Koester, eds, *Luther on Hermeneutics and the Gospel of Matthew* (Leipzig: Lutheran World Federation/Evangelische Verlangsanstalt, 2015), pp. 153-168, at p.163.

[30] Paul M. Joyce and Diana Lipton, *Lamentations Through the Centuries* (Chichester: Wiley-Blackwell, 2013) pp.88-90 (a volume in a new series not simply of 'reception history' but of 'reception exegesis'). See also Brant Pitre, *Jesus and the Jewish Roots of Mary: Unveiling the Mother of the Messiah* (New York, N.Y.: Image, 2018), pp. 183-184.

[31] Sayers, *Man Born to be King*, p. 92.

[32] Sayers, *Man Born to be King*, p. 288.

[33] Sayers, *Man Born to be King*, pp. 294-295.

[34] Sayers, *Man Born to be King*, p. 312, p. 289. See also the Kathe Kollwitz sculpture, 'Mother and Dead Son'/Pieta in Berlin's Neue Wache memorial to the victims of tyranny, https://theculturetrip.com>Berlin>Art, accessed 2.1.10.

[35] Dorothy L. Sayers, *The Just Vengeance. The Lichfield Festival Play for 1946* (Eugene, Ore.: Wipf and Stock, 2011). For a new reading, see Frances Clemson, 'Doing Justice to the Past: Time, Drama and Peacebuilding', in Jolyon Mitchell, Giselle Vincette, Theodora Hawksley and Hal Cuthbertson, eds, *Peacebuilding and the Arts* (London: Palgrave Macmillan, 2020), pp. 415-433.

[36] Some 55, 573 men died in UK Bomber Command alone, apart from those who died in the US Army Air Force.

[37] Sayers, *Man Born to be King*, p.36.

[38] Her translation of *Hell* (London: Penguin, 1949) appeared in the new Penguin Classics series, and was awarded a University of Durham D.Litt. degree in 1950 (the year of the Papal promulgation of the Dogma of the Assumption of Mary). Just five years later she published the second part, *Purgatory.*

[39] The *Paradise* volume published after the death of Dorothy L. Sayers in 1957, was almost entirely the work of Dr Barbara Reynolds who had known Dorothy L. Sayers since 1946. (London: Penguin, 1962); see Canto 7:19, p.108. Dr Reynolds in her turn received the D.Litt. Degree from Durham in 1995 both for her own work in Italian Studies and for the major contribution she had made both to Dante studies in her own right and in her collaborations with Dorothy L. Sayers which took many forms.

[40] *Paradise* (London: Penguin, 1962), p. 343.

[41] The whole prayer was the only complete section of the *Paradise* volume available to Dr Reynolds for incorporation into her translation and commentary.

[42] *The Just Vengeance,* pp. 69-70, p.89, pp. 93-95, pp. 97-98.

[43] Evelyn Underhill, *The Golden Sequence* (London Methuen, 1932); *Abba. Meditations on the Lord's Prayer* (London: Longmans, Green, 1940); Dorothy L. Sayers, 'Pentecost' in her *The Mind of the Maker* (London: Methuen, 1940), pp. 88-99.

[44] See James MacMillan, *A Scots Song: A Life of Music* (Edinburgh: Birlinn, 2019); James MacMillan, 'The Most Spiritual of the Arts: Music, Modernity, and the Search for the Sacred,' in George Corbett ed., *Annunciations: Sacred Music for the Twenty-First Century* (Cambridge: Open Book Publishers, 2019), pp. 9-16, and George Corbett, 'Mary as a Model for Creative People: Establishing Theologian Composer Partnerships with James MacMillan', pp.31-36. For MacMillan's own compositions, see also St Salvator's Chapel Choir, *Annunciations: Sacred Music for the 21st Century,* St Salvator's Chapel Choir and Sean Heath, conducted by Tom Wilkinson (Sanctiandree, SAN0006, 2018), http://stsalvatorschapelchoir.wp.st-andrews.ac.k/recordings/.

[45] Both MacMillan and Paul Mealor have found writing the 'Stabat Mater' inescapable: see Margaret McKcKerron with Paul Mealor, 'The Surrogate Priest: Reflecting on Vocation with Welsh Composer Paul Mealor', in George Corbett, ed., *Annunciations: Sacred Music for the Twenty-First Century* (Cambridge: Open Book Publishers, 2019), pp.17-29. See also Howard Blake, 'Christmas Hope,' Track 17 on SIGCD202 Hyperion, 'Four Songs of the Nativity' (Naxos 8572453) and 'The Passion of Mary,' Op.577, Dec.2006, Highbridge Music Ltd. In a different mode, see Stephanie A. Budwey, *Sing of Mary: Giving Voice to Marian Theology and Devotion* (Collegeville, Minn.: Liturgical Press, 2014).

[46] The United Church of Christ (USA) Press production (with different editorial teams) *Imagining the Word: An Arts and Lectionary Resource* in three vols. (Cleveland, Ohio: United Church Press, 1994, 1995,1996); on the Benedictine *St John's Bible* (https://www.saintjohnsbible.org/), see Michael Patella, *Word and Image: The Hermeneutics of the St John's Bible* (Collegeville Minn.: Liturgical Press, 2013) which attends to art as 'embodiment of theological thinking, wonderment, and exploration' (p.xiv). Patella also writes on enjoyment as 'itself a spiritual and theological virtue which can also lead to greater theological and spiritual insight' (p.75). Compare Trevor Hart, 'Protestantism and the Arts', in Alister E. McGrath and Darren C. Marks, *The Blackwell Companion to Protestantism* (Oxford: Oxford University Press, 2004), pp. 268-286. See also Martin Warner, 'The Image of Mary', *International Journal for the Study of the Christian Church* 4 (2004): 207-219 and Jane Heath, 'Mary's Image as Theology', in Mark McIvoy, Casey Strine and Alexis Torrance, eds, *Image as Theology: Arts and the Sacred vol.5* (Turnhout: Brepols, 2020).

[47] Annemarie C. Mayer, 'Mary—"Mother of the Church": Challenging Conciliar Ecclesiology', *International Journal for the Study of the Christian Church* 15 (2015): 186-198. See also Robin M. Jenson, '*Mater Ecclesia* and *Fons Aeterna: The Church and Her Womb in Ancient Christian Tradition*', in Amy-Jill Levine and Maria Mayo Robbins, eds, *A Feminist Companion to Patristic Literature* (London: T & T Clark, 2008), pp. 137-155; Ann Maria

Laato, 'Biblical Mothers as images of the Church: The Birth of Eve as an Image of the Birth of the Church', *International Journal for the Study of the Christian Church* 19 (2019): 44-58.
[48] See Evelyn Underhill, 'Catholic Worship: Western and Eastern' in *Worship* pp.186-209, and her attention to the ikon, 'a special vehicle of grace to the particular person for whose use it is blessed', not least an ikon of the Blessed Virgin.
[49] E.g. Sarah Jane Boss, 'Mary', in Adrian Hastings, Alistair Mason and Hugh Pyper, eds, *The Oxford Companion to Christian Thought* (Oxford: Oxford University Press, 2000), pp. 414-416; Tina Beattie, 'Mary and Spirituality', in Philip Sheldrake, ed., *The New SCM Dictionary of Christian Spirituality* (London: SCM Press, 2005), pp. 424-426. Compare the latter's response to David Brown, 'Mary and Virgin promise' on 'discipleship imaginatively relived…awaiting its realization' in Brown's *Discipleship and Imagination. Christian Tradition and Truth* (Oxford: Oxford University Press, 2000), pp. 226-287, at p. 287, in her essay 'From Ethics to Eschatology: the Continuing Validity of the New Eve for Christian Doctrine and Discipleship', in Robert MacSwain and Taylor Worley, eds, *Theology Aesthetics and Culture: Responses to the Work of David Brown* (Oxford: Oxford University Press, 2012), pp. 64-78, and the point that 'Mary symbolizes the perfection of the new creation, the end of Eve's suffering, and the fulfilment of God's promise of redemption' (p.73); as well as Andrew Louth on the possible recovery of 'a concern for single-mindedness and simplicity, of which virginity was a physical and social expression', in 'Virgin Birth' in Adrian Hastings, Alistair Mason and Hugh Pyper, eds, *Oxford Companion to Christian Thought*.
[50] See David Brown's 'reply' in Garrick V. Allen, Christopher R. Brewer and Dennis F. Kinlaw III, eds., *The Moving Text: Interdisciplinary Perspectives on David Brown and the Bible* (London: SCM Press, 2018), p. 222. See also Brittany E. Wilson, 'Mary and Her Interpreters,' in Carol. A Newsom, Sharon H. Ringe, and Jacqueline E. Lapsley, eds., *The Women's Bible Commentary Revised and Updated* (Louisville, Kenn.: Westminster John Knox Press, 2012), pp. 512-516.
[51] For example, Amy-Jill Levine, *The Misunderstood Jew: the Church and the Scandal of the Jewish Jesus* (New York, N.Y.: Harper, 2006), pp.196-199. David J. Lasher, 'Mary in Jewish Tradition,' in Amy-Jill Levine and Marc Zvi Brettler eds, *The Jewish Annotated New Testament* (New York, N.Y.: Oxford University Press, 2011), pp. 744-747 writes about the repulsion associated with Mary because of the crimes against Jews committed in the name of both her and her son, but also a kind of fascination with positive aspects of her character. John Darr, 'Belittling Mary: Insult, Humiliations and Early Developments in Mariology', in Christine E. Joynes and Christopher C. Rowland, eds., *From the Margins 2: Women of the New Testament and their Afterlives* (Sheffield: Sheffield Phoenix Press, 2009), pp. 24-39, writes of how Mary was caught in the cross-fire of insult and response to it as nascent Christianity fought for its identity. See also John F. A. Sawyer, 'Isaiah and the Jews' in Sawyer's *The Fifth Gospel: Isaiah in the History of Christianity* (Cambridge: Cambridge University Press, 1996), pp. 100-125, which examines some of the lamentable history of anti-Jewish polemic, whilst in his chapter 'Women and Isaiah' Sawyer makes the point that in Isaiah 7.14 it is the young woman who calls her son 'Immanuel', she herself standing for faith and strength of character. The recent Church of England Faith and Order Commission, *God's Unfailing Word: Theological and Practical Perspectives on Christian-Jewish Relations* (London: Church House Publications, 2019) ignores texts and traditions about Mary. Illuminating commentary may be found in the Feminist Companion to the Bible Series and the New Cambridge Bible Commentary series, of which a notable example is the Jewish-Christian volume written jointly by Amy-Jill Levine and Ben Witherington III, *The Gospel of Luke* (Cambridge: Cambridge University Press, 2018), engaging with 'the same text through different lenses: Jewish and Christian (of particular sorts)' (p.17).
[52] Margaret Barker, 'Isaiah', in James G. D. Dunn and John W. Rogerson eds, *Eerdmans Commentary on the Bible* (Grand Rapids, MI: Eerdmans, 2003), pp. 489-542, especially her

comments on ch.7 and 49, pp. 505-506, 531-533. For her own summaries of her publications see www.margaretbarker.com.

[53] See Margaret Barker, *The Mother of the Lord Vol.1: The Lady in the Temple* (London: Bloomsbury, 2012), especially 'Losing the Lady', pp. 329-374 and 'The Lady of the Church', p.375. The recovered scrolls of Qumran provide further illumination.

[54] See especially 'The Setting' and Other Voices' in Margaret Barker, *Christmas: The Original Story* (London: SPCK, 2008), pp. 1-49, and on the Qur'an, pp. 162-175. See also Jaroslav Pelikan, *Mary through the Centuries: Her Place in the History of Culture* (New Haven, Conn.: Yale University Press,1996), pp. 67-79 on 'The Heroine of the Qur'an and the Black Madonna'. Pelikan also draws attention to the Latin translation of Prov. 31.10: 'A woman of valour who can find?' p.91, pp. 177-188. And 'You are the splendour and honour of your people/ you are the highest glory of your race, and the supreme renown of an ancient house', in John Nassichuk, 'Biblical Elegy and *Quattrocento* Marian Enconium: Marantonio Sabellico's *Carmina De Beata Virgine Maria*', in Diane Apostlolos-Cappadona, ed., *Biblical Women and the Arts: Biblical Reception 5* (London: T & T Clark, 2018), pp.143-157, at p.157; Natasha O'Hear, 'Picturing the Woman Clothed with the Sun (Revelation 12): Images of Apocalyptic Conflict, Piety and Strength', includes discussion of Marian images by Mexican-American women, infusing Mary with energy and fortitude, pp. 203-228. On 'theophany' see e.g. Margaret Barker, *The Risen Lord* (Edinburgh: T & T Clark, 1996), pp.52-55, pp. 92-110; and Madhavi Nevader, 'The Gods Talk to Men: Reading Mary with the Annunciations of the Hebrew Bible and the Ancient Near East', in George Corbett, ed., *Annunciations: Sacred Music for the Twenty-First Century* (Cambridge: Open Book Publishers, 2019), pp. 45-55: 'God talks to women' in relation to an 'expansive hinterland of texts', pp.54-55.

[55] Thomas Arentzen, *The Virgin in Song: Mary and the Poetry of Romanos the Melodist* (Philadelphia, Penn.: University of Pennsylvania Press, 2017), p.8.

[56] For the text in translation following the Greek original, see Arentzen, *The Virgin in Song*, pp. 181-187, and explication, pp.58-84.

[57] Arentzen, *The Virgin in Song*, pp.130-134

[58] Margaret Barker, 'Wisdom Imagery and the Mother of God', in Leslie Brubaker and Mary B. Cunningham, eds, *The Cult of the Mother of God in Byzantium: Texts and Images* (Farnham: Ashgate, 2011), pp. 91-106.

[59] Barker, 'Wisdom Imagery and the Mother of God', p.107. See also Krasta Banev, " Myriad of Names to Represent Her Nobleness" : The Church and the Virgin Mary in the Psalms and Hymns of Byzantium', in Justin A. Mihoc and Leonard Aldea, eds., *A Celebration of Living Theology* (London: Bloomsbury, 2014), pp. 75-103; Andrew Louth, 'John of Damascus on the Mother of God as a Link between Humanity and God, in Leslie Brubaker and Mary B. Cunningham, eds, *The Cult of the Mother of God in Byzantium: Texts and Images* (Farnham: Ashgate, 2011), pp. 154-161; Andrew Louth, 'Mary the Mother of God and Ecclesiology: Some Orthodox Reflections', *International Journal for the Study of the Christian Church* 18 (2018): 132-145, p.132. None of these Orthodox theologians so far seem to draw on Margaret Barker's work.

[60] See Jeffrey Taylor, ed., *Robert Heindel: An Exhibition of his Paintings inspired by David Bintley's Ballet to the Music of John Tavener* (London: The Gallery, Cock Street, 1999).

[61] See Serene Jones, 'Sin, Creativity and the Christian Life: Rachel and Mary in Traumatic Embrace', in her *Trauma and Grace. Theology in a Ruptured World* (Louisville, Kenn.: Westminster John Knox Press, 2009), pp. 101-125; David Peters, *Post-Traumatic God: How the Church Cares for People who have been to Hell and Back* (New York, N.Y.: Morehouse, 2016); Shelley Rambo, *Resurrecting Wounds: Living in the Aftermath of Trauma* (Waco, Tex.: Baylor University Press, 2017).

[62] Karen O'Donnell, *Broken Bodies. The Eucharist, Mary and the Body in Trauma Theology* (London: SCM Press, 2018). See further, Karen O'Donnell and Katie Cross, eds, *Feminist*

Trauma Theologies. Body, Scripture and Church in Critical Perspective (London: SCM Press, 2020).
[63] O'Donnell, *Broken Bodies*, pp.6-8.
[64] O'Donnell, *Broken Bodies*, pp.189-191. And see Linda L. Layne, '"True Gifts from God": Paradoxes of Motherhood, Sacrifice, and Enrichment' in *Motherhood Lost: A Feminist Account of Pregnancy Loss in America* (London: Routledge, 2003) which includes the suffering of both parents, though not explicitly the experience of e.g. carrying the coffin of a still-born child or one born with a condition which will mean heartbreaking early death.
[65] O'Donnell, *Broken Bodies*, pp.161-162, p.194.
[66] O'Donnell, *Broken Bodies*, pp. 90-91. The kind of material included pp.94-104 on Marian typology could well benefit from engagement with Margaret Barker's work and Orthodox tradition.
[67] O'Donnell, *Broken Bodies*, pp. pp.167-169, 175-179.
[68] O'Donnell, *Broken Bodies*, pp. p.197, p.203.
[69] Karen O'Donnell has since identified with Anglicanism.

7

Annunciation: A Sermon

Over the Sundays of Advent we hear and read from each of the Gospels which became authorised for Christians in the first few centuries of the Christian era. We hear and read from all four because each of them make two points of central importance in different ways. The first point is that Jesus of Nazareth had and has an exceptional indeed unique relationship to God whose world it is, despite many appearances to the contrary. And the second is that Jesus' proclamation of the reign of God was to begin closely associated with that of a kinsman, son of a priestly household, whose name was John, by whom Jesus himself was baptised. Each gospel writer attempts to make sense of what Christian communities are to make of all this as they form and live under Roman rule and occupation as illegal groups of worshippers, possibly troublesome to the authorities and certainly with internal difficulties to negotiate as converts from quite different backgrounds join these communities. So, suppose that somewhere in the Roman East a member of one of these communities, a writer of exceptional gifts, Greek speaking, thoroughly familiar with Jewish scripture in Greek, the common speech of the day, suppose this writer—call him Luke according to tradition —either discovers or has sent to him a copy of a most valuable text : the gospel of Mark. There he finds that in just a few short sharp sentences Mark identifies Jesus of Nazareth not simply as an anointed one—a Messiah—but as Son of God—the language of royalty, of kingship. And Mark goes straight to the proclamation of John the Baptist as the forerunner of Jesus who turns up for baptism by him. What is Luke to make of all this in his turn? Is there not more to be said, to be explored and explained on both counts—Jesus' relation to God and Jesus' relation to John? So, with incomparable skill, Luke writes his own narrative, beginning with John, the slightly older of the two men.

John, as he makes unambiguously clear, is son of parents both of whom are from families committed to the worship of the re-built magnificent temple in Jerusalem, both of them devout, but childless, and getting past the age when a much-longed for male child might be born to them. Zacharias has the special privilege of taking his turn at burning incense in the sanctuary of the temple, where he has a distinctly unnerving experience. God of course, as Zacharias knows, may manifest himself in different ways, depending on circumstances. In our first reading from 1 Samuel, the manifestation of God is mediated through a prophet, Nathan, commissioned by God to instruct king David that his line will continue for ever, indeed that God will be father to David's son and his descendants. And David's son will replace the tabernacle David has built to house God's throne—replace it with a temple. The Davidic line and the worship conducted in that temple are most carefully related to one another. David of course is anything but a moral exemplar, any more than others of his line—that is not the point. The point is that he is portrayed as utterly and passionately devoted to God and trusting in the divine promise. So fast-forward to Zacharias, for through and well beyond utter disaster, David's city of Jerusalem has been re-established and a new temple has been built within it. There Zacharias is to be found by Gabriel, not a prophet like Nathan, but this time God in angelic presence.

Gabriel has been met with before in the experience of the visionary Daniel at the time of evening prayer in a time and place of utter desolation and exile, when Gabriel comes to instruct Daniel—addressed as 'greatly beloved' (Gabriel always devastatingly courteous!) who reminds him of that promise to David about the divine reign and the worship of the temple, eventually rebuilt as we have recalled. Zacharias as it were takes Gabriel on—how is he to believe in the divine gift of a son; how is Zacharias to *know* this and to believe the promises of his son's role in relation to the divine reign? The result of that question is that he is struck dumb, so at the completion of his responsibility for the burning of incense on that occasion all he can do is gesture rather than actually pronounce blessing to the assembled worshippers. But Gabriel is indeed to be trusted, for Elizabeth's child is conceived and safely born and named by his father.

In the meantime, as it were, Gabriel turns his attention elsewhere, out of Jerusalem, out of that centre of devotion, up north to Galilee, to a woman betrothed to a man called Joseph, himself briefly identified as of the Davidic line—Joseph is of course given attention in Matthew's Gospel. The angel greets Mary in words which recall the 'greatly beloved' greeting to Daniel. The Greek means something like 'Good day to you, God's good to you', or 'God indeed favours you'. Some texts add in at this point 'Blessed are you among women'—the words found on the lips of Elizabeth when Mary visits her and so to speak transferred to Gabriel's greeting to reinforce the meaning of his greeting. I'll come back to those words in a moment. Mary, like Daniel, like Zacharias, unsurprisingly does not initially know what to make of this greeting 'God's good to you'—she might well be much troubled by it, but Gabriel explains that divine goodness, divine favour, means a son for her who will be 'Son of the Highest', who will inherit those promises made to David. Mary also takes Gabriel on; in making the obvious comment—she is indeed betrothed, but she does not yet cohabit with Joseph as we might say. And of course, she has a point, for as in the case of other women in scripture who are the predecessors of Elizabeth and Mary, the divine promise of a child does not exclude human fatherhood. But it's clear to Luke at any rate, that in this instance a male progenitor is not involved—so the words 'I will be his father and he shall be my son' of the divine promise to David now take on a new meaning, however crucial Joseph is to be in the life of Mary's son. Mary accepts the knowledge and significance of Elizabeth's pregnancy—nothing is impossible to God, and affirms her own status as 'slave' of God (a *doulos* to her *Kurios*, her Lord) - 'handmaiden' and 'servant' softens it—with all the consequences that may follow that admission, and she cannot possibly know what that may entail.

So: she is clearly separated from Joseph for a time, for she heads off to visit Elizabeth in her home near Jerusalem, and Elizabeth too becomes a prophet in her turn, and acknowledges Mary as 'Blessed among women'. We miss the significance of these words unless we recall that two other women have been so addressed. One of them, Jael, destroys the fugitive Philistine commander, Sisera to whom she has given shelter and hospitality (Judges 4-5), and in a different narrative, Judith has destroyed Holofernes (Judith 13/16). The point is that they were called 'blessed' because they destroyed those thwarting the divine reign as enemies of God's people. It is not that Mary may be required to fulfil an equally terrible task, but that like them, she's a woman of courage—something at least one poet, Denise Levertov, spotted in her reflections on this episode—a point usually missed by commentators focussed on Mary's consent / obedience/ submission as a 'slave' of God. Her confession does not make her a nonentity—anything but. And Luke at this juncture as it were re-writes the song of praise of Hannah, the mother of Samuel (1 Sam. 2) in voicing Mary's prophetic confidence and courage in the praise of God familiar to us as the 'Magnificat': 'My soul magnifies the Lord'.

Thus, Luke has addressed himself to the conviction that Jesus has a special relationship to God, and that he has kith and kin in the priestly family into which John is born. He also tells us that Jesus' parents take their child to the Passover feast each year in Jerusalem, surely visiting their kin there, because when the twelve year old Jesus goes missing they know where to start looking for him—among their kin and acquaintances, and eventually locate him in the temple learning from the teachers there and quizzing them about what they have to say. The implication surely is that he learns a great deal from John and his family. And John, as we see, turns his back on the temple, and chooses the life of a prophet relocated on the river Jordan, with baptism, not worship in the temple, as the sign of renewal and repentance needed in respect of the divine reign. There too was Jesus initially to be found, closely identified with John's teaching and practice, and Luke tells us that Jesus heads back to Galilee only when John is arrested and of course killed—Jesus finding his own extraordinary place in relation to God's reign, whilst also returning to the great feasts in Jerusalem and its temple—with which he remains both engaged and yet critically engaged, as his later accusers well knew.

What, finally, of Mary in Luke's gospel, given her courage in accepting Gabriel's message of divine goodness and favour, whatever that might entail? Luke has something to offer about Mary beyond that initial annunciation, for in his gospel she becomes one of those, with others of Jesus' kin, who listen to him, believe him and act on his words, and crucially in Luke's second book on the acts of the apostles—(those who respond to all that happens)—give us a brief but very important glimpse of Mary which we easily overlook. For he places her explicitly named, with her kin and Jesus' disciples, in Jerusalem, at the heart of the worship of God. As a consequence, familiar though we are with paintings and poetry of Gabriel's annunciation to Mary, we should recall that all the earliest representations of Pentecost —the Spirit given to that early community of believers - all have Mary at the centre of the picture. Spirit-endowed at annunciation, and Spirit—endowed at Pentecost—as she so still appears in the ikons of the Orthodox churches. Luke believes, of course, that God's resurrection of his Son means that the promises made to David are now made as it were open to all, with God's Son now the one who himself bestows his Spirit on believers. So in effect there is not just one annunciation, but two, as Luke would have his community believe: and Mary is central to both.

This sermon was preached at All Saints Scottish Episcopal Church, St Andrews.

8

The Royal Mail

Starlight, starbright, shining and sparkling, God's cloak of honour and majesty, in heavens stretched out like a curtain! (Psalm 104:1-2). From this realm of divine splendour God sends angel-messengers who wing their way on missions of blessing to find people longing to know what to make of their lives. The shepherd boys and men who live and work out of doors in all weathers, caring for and defending their sheep—they sometimes catch just a glimpse of one of these winged messengers amongst the light and colours of the sky.

It is possible for someone to refuse a blessing, if what it means seems to ask too much, in an uncertain and maybe dangerous future. But angel-messenger Gabriel finds the right person, a very young woman, Mary, committed to her much-loved future husband, Joseph. The angel greets her: 'God's good to you!' She will need to hear and believe that, given the proposed blessing of becoming mother to a specially God-sent son, a saviour from hurts and harm. Will Joseph stand by her? She summons up all her courage and says 'Yes'! Safely born, her little son already knows her heartbeat. Now he knows her face, her eyes, her smile, her voice as she talks to him, feeds him and cares for him. He smiles back as she sings to him her own song of joy in the mercy and promises of God (Luke 1: 46-55). And the baby delights in Joseph and all that he too does for him.

Joseph of Nazareth wants only the good for Mary, whom he loves and trusts. The last thing he wants to do is to abandon her to disgrace and danger. 'O send out thy light and thy truth: let them lead me', he prays (Psalm 43:3), and commits himself to Mary and her unborn child. His first task is to get the pair of them to Bethlehem (his ancestral city) to register with the Roman authorities for tax. Then he has to find somewhere secure and starlit for the birth of the child she carries. In any event, a stable is much better than a noisy, crowded inn. And it is kept warm by the working animals of the household. 'The ox knoweth its owner, and the ass his master's crib' (Isaiah 1:3). They are curious about the baby, and some of them will help the family flee for safety.

There are others who hear about and want to see this baby too. Shepherds trust the goodness and mercy of God (Psalm 23), but on nearby fields under the starlight they are almost overwhelmed by the glory of God, seeing and hearing first one angel and then a host of them in celebration. They proclaim peace and goodwill for all, the promise brought with the birth of the child. Some shepherds go to see the baby and his family for themselves, and what they have seen they report to others. The news begins to spread (Luke 2:8-18).

Stranger visitors are royal seekers of wisdom, who also watch the stars wheeling in the heavens, hoping to find a meaning in what they see. They follow one splendid star especially, and bring magnificent gifts to the family (Isaiah 60:3). They soon realise that knowledge of their visit, their presence and their gifts will almost certainly bring danger to the inn and its stable, and quietly find a route back to their own countries. Joseph may well be thankful for their gifts, for he must now take Mary and the child out of harm's reach. With their animals they trust to the starlit night to find their way, and flee for refuge down to Egypt. Well may they pray: 'The Lord is my light and my salvation; whom shall I fear? The Lord is the strength of my life; of whom shall I be afraid?' (Psalm 27:1).

This text accompanied the Royal Mail's Christmas stamps 2019.

9

Assumption: A Sermon

Today's commemoration and celebration of the Blessed Virgin Mary has to do with a feast that has deep roots in the church, both east and west. Let us recall, to begin with, that there have for centuries been such commemorations and celebrations of the saints on the days on which they died, or were deemed to have died. The framework for such feasts is to be found in the phrase 'the communion of saints' in the Apostles' Creed, and in the last clause of the Nicene Creed, which affirms belief in God the Spirit and Life-Giver; the Church, into which we are bodily joined in baptism; in forgiveness; and in resurrection and new life. Christ is no solitary—risen, ascended and glorified, he draws to himself redeemed humanity into the company of heaven, into the exuberance and delight of a repossessed paradise. And it makes sense, in that company to think of his mother being given a special place of honour.

So in the Orthodox family of churches, 15 August is the Feast of Mary's Dormition, her falling asleep. Look at representations of her death, and you see her surrounded by Christ's grieving disciples, whilst Christ himself receives her into his arms as newborn into life with him. In the churches of Latin origin, 15 August has been kept as the feast of Mary's Assumption, her being received into glory, blessed and graced as ever, and finally transformed by God. It is notoriously difficult to paint Christ's own resurrection and ascension, and the same point has to be made about attempts to depict Mary's Assumption, her being taken up into heaven. The emphasis in east and west—Dormition or Assumption—has been and clearly remains different, but let us identify the fundamental point that each have in common. And this is that Mary's Dormition or Assumption is one sign, and arguably a crucial sign, of Christ's own continuing humanity, a presence continually available to us in Spirit and sacrament; and also a crucial sign of the promise and gracious blessing and transformation of our own lives. So it is entirely appropriate that this celebration takes place in mid-august, a time of great beauty, fruition and fulfilment, associated with the abundance of flowers and plants, especially plants and herbs of healing, once upon a time brought into church on this day.

So why did this feast disappear from so many churches including what became the Anglican Communion, at the time of the Reformation? Why are we discovering it anew, as on this occasion? One answer lies in the fact of its being made a dogma in the Roman Catholic Church in 1950 and in ecumenical response recovered in the Anglican Communion world-wide from about 1970 onwards. Let us briefly recall some of the concerns of those who saw the desperate need for the reform of the Church in the west several centuries ago. Reformers protested especially against whatsoever seemed to obscure the priority and centrality of Christ's redemptive work; they were concerned about the relative weight to be given to Scripture and developing tradition; and they were deeply disturbed about the pretensions and political competence and incompetence of an over triumphalist church. An essential point for them was to understand that salvation was wholly dependent on God's gracious initiative. Anything that seemed to obscure that simply had to go, and included much devotion associated with Mary. Yet in the Book of Common Prayer, for instance, much remained which drew attention back to Mary. Take the feast of Christ's own Nativity, with its profoundly Trinitarian collect: 'Almighty God who hast given us thy only-begotten Son to take our nature upon him, and as at this time to be born of a pure Virgin; grant that we being regenerate, and made thy children by adoption and grace, may daily be renewed by thy Holy Spirit...'. The feasts of Annunciation and Purification were retained, and given more weight than the feasts of Mary's own Conception and Nativity. And that latter feast of Mary's Nativity, celebrated on 8 September, has for many Anglicans world-wide, remained the principal feast of Mary. So why did the feast of the Assumption disappear?

Recall, to begin with, the collect for All Saints' Day, which addresses God as the one 'who has knit together thine elect in one communion in the mystical body of thy Son, Christ our Lord ...'. No saint, not even Mary, is named. For what the reformers were trying to kill off was a particular mistake about the invocation of saints. The saints were most emphatically not to be invoked, if that meant that believers thought they could not approach Christ directly, and if that meant that the saints, and Mary in particular, could aid believers independently of Christ. I think we know this sort of problem; he's short of 'person skills'; he's difficult; he's busy; he might not understand; he's hopeless at listening. Have you tried his P.A., have you talked to his mother? If that's the way we think of Christ and his relationship to the company of heaven and to his mother, raised to glory, clearly something has gone very badly wrong, something the reformers were trying to put right.

And yet: a tradition of devotion to Mary survived among clergy and laity, as though, quite rightly, there is a sense in which we cannot understand Christ without catching hold of something of his relationship with his mother. There is something here which cannot be glimpsed unless we pay attention. Take John Donne, Dean of St Paul's in the seventeenth century, who wrote in one of his poems, 'A Litanie' about Mary: 'As her deeds were / our helps, so are her prayers, nor can she sue in vaine, who hath such titles unto you'. Donne wants his prayer to be associated with hers, and it is in that sense, and only in that sense, that he invokes her. And if we ask which biblical text in particular sustained devotion to Mary throughout the centuries, we would have to say that passage of Luke's gospel (1:46-55; and see also Hannah's Song in 1 Sam. 2; and Isaiah 61:10-11), and as the *Magnificat*, said or sung daily, a song which could well celebrate resurrection and transformation. In other words, with roots deep in Hebrew tradition, Scripture itself insistently reminded its readers and hearers that attention to Mary was to be sustained. But it has to be sustained with some discretion, so today is simply dedicated to the Blessed Virgin Mary—discretion surely taken too far if no further indications are given, let alone the recollection that churches and institutions in the past dedicated to Mary were to Mary of the feast of the Assumption!

In our times we have to move beyond the legacy of the reformers, and renegotiate differences and divergencies which stem from varying understandings of both Scripture and tradition. So the Anglican-Roman Catholic International commission agreed that 'Mary, the mother of God incarnate (*Theotokos*), was prepared by divine grace to be the mother of our Redeemer by whom she was herself redeemed, and received up into glory'. The problem then is for church communities to find ways of finding out what this might mean to them in their worshipping life! At the least, with the feast back in our calendar, we can explore its significance in hymns and newly written prayers as well as drawing on the rich liturgical and musical and artistic traditions of the past as well as the present.

So by celebrating this feast, what might we be committed to saying? Let's try this: Mary must have been exceptional in the way she lived in relation to

God and others, so that she could respond in freedom and delight to God's initiative. She is no 'doormat', clearly, for when an angelic presence greets her with 'Good day to you, God's good to you', she quizzes the archangel, takes him on, and responds with courage and generosity. In turn, she makes her son uniquely free for the full expression of God's life in him. That does not mean that all was sweetness and light between them—there are quite enough indications in the gospels to rid us of that kind of sentimentality, especially as his family realise that unless they can rein him in and get him home, he may well bring disaster not only on himself but on family and village as well. In the Gospels we find Christ's struggle to find his own vocation and the echoes of Mary's struggle too. She had her own share of grief at his experience of hideous betrayal and death, and yet is to be found at the very centre of the disciples at Pentecost (Acts 1:14). From the earliest representations of Pentecost from the sixth century onwards, it is there that we find her until in the post-Reformation period she disappears from view, despite being the only person in Scripture twice Spirit-graced. Her place is beautifully caught in the third stanza of one of our hymns ('Sing we of the blessed mother') where Mary with the disciples receives from on high 'the blazing glory of the Spirit's presence'. So Christ, we affirm, became and remains incarnate 'from the Holy Spirit and the Virgin Mary', the Spirit who is the giver of life, who gave and gives life to her and to us. So we can thank God for her and honour her 'raised on high and crowned with grace', and pray with her that her Son, the world's redeemer, will indeed 'grant us all to see his face'.

This sermon was preached at St Paul's Cathedral, London.

Acknowledgements

The author, editor and publisher are grateful to the following for permission to reprint copyright material.

Bloodaxe for lines from 'On the Mystery of the Incarnation' by Denise Levertov. From *A Door in the Hive, with Evening Train* by Denise Levertov (Newcastle upon Tyne: Bloodaxe Books, 1993).

Bloomsbury for reuse of material in 'The Nativity in Recent British Poetry' by Ann Loades. From *New Perspectives on the Nativity* edited by Jeremy Corley (London: T & T Clark, 2009). T & T Clark is an imprint of Bloomsbury Publishing Plc.

Alla Renée Bozarth for lines from 'Before Jesus—*Mary, Protopriest of the New Covenant*'. From *Accidental Wisdom* by Alla Renée Bozarth (iUniverse, 2003) and *This is My Body - Praying for Earth, Prayers from the Heart* by Alla Renée Bozarth (iUniverse, 2004)
http://allabozarthwordsandimages.blogspot.com/2011/12/i-cant-wait-for-christmas.html

Enitharmon Press for lines from 'The Three Stars: A Prophecy' by David Gascoyne. From *New Collected Poems* by David Gascoyne (London: Enitharmon Press, 2014) https://enitharmon.co.uk/product/new-collected-poems-david-gascoyne/
Copyright © Estate of David Gascoyne (literary executor, Stephen Stuart-Smith).

Gracewing for reuse of material in 'Feminist Theology: A View of Mary' by Ann Loades. From *Mary is for Everyone: Essays on Mary and Ecumenism* edited by William McLoughlin and Jill Pinnock (Leominster: Gracewing, 1997).

HarperCollins Australia for lines from 'Night and the Child' by Judith Wright. From Judith Wright, Collected Poems, first published in Australia in 1994 by Angus & Robertson, an imprint of HarperCollins Publishers Australia Pty Limited. The current in print edition was published in 2016 by HarperCollins Publishers Australia Pty Limited, ABN 36 009 913 517 harpercollins.com.au Copyright © The Estate of Judith Wright, 1994.

Sheffield Phoenix for reuse of material in 'Mary: Bone of Contention' by Ann Loades. From *From the Margins 2: Women of the New Testament and their Afterlives* edited by Christine E. Joynes and Christopher C. Rowland (Sheffield: Sheffield Phoenix Press, 2009).

David Higham for lines from 'I The Fear' and from 'The Annunciation' by Elizabeth Jennings. From *Collected Poems* by Elizabeth Jennings Manchester: Carcanet, 1986).

John Murray Press for lines from 'The Golden Door: The Three Kings' by George Mackay Brown. From *Collected Poems* by George Mackay Brown, edited by Archie Bevan and Brian Murray (London: John Murray, 2006).

Wiley-Blackwell for reuse of material in 'XX Mariological Marian International Congress, Rome 2000. The Position of the Anglican Communion regarding the Trinity and Mary' by Ann Loades. From *New Blackfriars* (82/967), 2001.

Every effort has been made to contact the copyright holders of other material cited.